SALTZBVRG

ANDREW STEPTOE

Mozart

EVERYMAN'S LIBRARY – EMI CLASSICS
MUSIC COMPANIONS

THIS IS A BORZOI BOOK

PUBLISHED BY ALFRED A. KNOPF, INC.

Copyright © 1997 by David Campbell Publishers Ltd.
and EMI Records Ltd.
Music compilation ℗ and © 1997 by EMI Classics (USA)
Text copyright © 1997 by Andrew Steptoe

ISBN 0-375-40001-X

Front endpaper: Plan of Salzburg: coloured engraving by Georg Braun
and Franz Hogenberg from *Civitates Orbis Terrarum*, Cologne
(AKG London).
Back endpaper: Bird's-eye view of Vienna (detail), engraved by Joseph
Daniel von Huber, *c.* 1770 (British Library, London:
Maps K4 TAB 40).
Frontispiece: Wolfgang Amadeus Mozart: oil painting by Barbara
Krafft, 1819 (AKG London: Gesellschaft der Musikfreunde,
Vienna).
Title page: Detail from Mozart's earliest composition, K1a–d, 1761
(The Pierpont Morgan Library, Mary Flagler Cary Music Collection
(CARY 201)/Art Resource, NY. The Pierpont Morgan Library,
New York, New York, USA).

Series General Editor: Michael Rose

Picture research by Helen Ottaway

Typeset in the UK by AccComputing, Castle Cary, Somerset
Printed and bound in Germany by Mohndruck Graphische Betriebe
GmbH, Gütersloh

Contents

A Note on Köchel Numbers

Mozart's musical output was so immense that a system for identifying particular works is essential. The task of making a chronological catalogue was first carried out, appropriately enough, by a botanist and mineralogist, Ludwig von Köchel. Köchel's catalogue has gone through numerous editions since its publication more than 130 years ago, and unfortunately many of the original numbers were chronologically inaccurate. Specialists often use the new Köchel numbers provided in the third or sixth editions. However, the original numbers are the best recognized and are used here, so references to Mozart's music are all accompanied by a 'K' number.

A Note on the Currency

The units of currency operating in the eighteenth century were complicated, with differences between countries and even regions or small states. For convenience, I have translated all currencies into the Viennese gulden (or florin). A gulden was made up of 60 kreutzer, and was equivalent during this period to about two English shillings.

Preface

Mozart's music is enjoying unprecedented popularity, and this apprecia-
tion of his work has been coupled with increased interest in his life. A
number of biographies have been written over the past two decades,
ranging from brief summaries to substantial academic tomes. I was
attracted to write this biography for two reasons. Firstly, I felt there was
a place for a short book that not only described Mozart's life and music,
but also placed it within the social and cultural context of the era. Too
often, composers are viewed in isolation from their times and experiences.
Secondly, I was intrigued by the possibilities of linking the text with
recordings of Mozart's music. One of the frustrations of writing about
composers is the difficulty of illustrating musically what one is describing
in words. The addition of the three compact discs greatly enhances the
potential for understanding the way Mozart's life and music are con-
nected. In choosing the music that accompanies this biography, I decided
not to select extracts from Mozart's most popular works or his 'greatest
hits'. Rather, I have chosen pieces that epitomize the types of composition
that were significant at different stages of his life. In addition, I have
included complete works as far as possible, since Mozart's pieces are best
appreciated in their entirety. Unfortunately, Mozart's stage works are too
long to be presented complete, so two of the finest operas are represented
by self-contained sections or sequences.

   I should like to take the opportunity to express my great thanks to
Michael Rose, General Editor of the series, for his patient support and
enthusiasm throughout this project. I am also indebted to Richard
Bradburn from EMI Classics, whose compendious knowledge of the
recorded catalogue facilitated the selection of the music. I am most
grateful to Helen Ottaway for her work in reseaching the illustrations
and to Margaret Reuben for invaluable clerical assistance. I owe most of
all to my family and friends who have provided unfailing encouragement.
This book is dedicated with my love to Lucy, William and Matthew.

18 April 1996

The Empress Maria Theresa with her husband Francis and their children on the terrace of Schönbrunn Palace. Mozart's patron, the future Emperor Joseph II, stands in the centre of the star pattern. Painted in 1750 by Martin van Meytens the younger.

CHAPTER 1
Europe in 1756

Mozart spent almost all his life in central Europe, first in the independent ecclesiastical state of Salzburg where he was brought up, and later in Vienna where he lived as an adult. Vienna was the capital of the Habsburg monarchy which was ruled at the time of Mozart's birth by Maria Theresa, and subsequently by her son Joseph II. Both these monarchs were to have a personal influence on the course of the composer's life.

The Habsburg lands were vast, as can be seen in the map on page 63. They constituted a monarchy rather than a kingdom, since technically they were composed of several individual kingdoms and duchies. They included most of present-day Austria, Bohemia, Moravia, Slovenia, Croatia, the vast lands of Hungary, Transylvania, parts of the Ukraine and Serbia, the Austrian Netherlands, and states in Italy including Lombardy (centred around Milan) and Tuscany. These domains were very diverse in culture, language and religion, making Vienna one of the most cosmopolitan cities in Europe. The Habsburg monarchs had also held the title of Holy Roman Emperor almost uninterruptedly for three centuries. The Holy Roman Empire (*Reich*) dated from the time of Charlemagne, but by the mid-eighteenth century was a loose amalgam of German secular and ecclesiastical states, together with about fifty self-governing free imperial cities such as Frankfurt. The landscape was dotted with minor courts, each with its cultural life, courtiers, legislature and social hierarchy. The emperor was elected by the rulers of six of the most powerful secular states (the electors of Saxony, Bavaria, Branden-burg, Hanover and the Palatinate, and the king of Bohemia), together with the archbishops of Mainz, Cologne and Trier.

The fact that the Habsburg monarch was also Holy Roman Emperor makes the power structure of central Europe confusing, as the two were by no means synonymous. As the map shows, large parts of the Habsburg

domains were outside the bounds of the empire. Conversely, by the eighteenth century, the Habsburgs exerted little power over the imperial states that were not parts of their own domain. Then in 1740, the continent was thrown into turmoil by the death of the Emperor Charles VI. His heir was his daughter Maria Theresa, and she duly became ruler of the monarchy. But his wish that she succeed him as empress was not respected, and the elector of Bavaria was pronounced Holy Roman Emperor. It was only after the War of the Austrian Succession that Maria Theresa's husband Francis Stephen of Lorraine was elected emperor, re-establishing the link between the Habsburg monarchy and the empire. After the death of Francis in 1765, Maria Theresa's son Joseph was elected emperor, and was made co-regent of the monarchy. Mother and son often disagreed, since Joseph was a progressive and his views were formed by the Enlightenment. Nevertheless, they ruled together until her death fifteen years later.

The political map of Europe was extraordinarily fluid during Mozart's time. The dominant state at the beginning of the century was France. France was the richest and most populous country, since the lands of central and eastern Europe were fragmented and still recovering from the ravages of the Thirty Years' War. However, the eighteenth century saw the rise of Prussia under the rule of Frederick the Great as a major European power, sponsored in large measure by Britain. The empires of Spain and Sweden collapsed, the Polish state was partitioned, and the focus of international rivalries shifted to domination of India and the rich American colonies. Within Europe itself, France had been the traditional enemy of the Habsburg monarchy for more than two centuries. But in the years immediately preceding Mozart's birth, there was a dramatic shift. The Austrians feared the rise of Prussia, which had successfully taken control of the large and rich Habsburg province of Silesia during the War of the Austrian Succession. A coalition between the Habsburg monarchy, France, Russia and Sweden was therefore formed in 1756, precipitating the Seven Years' War against Prussia and her British allies.

These events may have been of great significance for the future of the continent, but many people remained ignorant of the manoeuvres and postures of the great states. Communication was still primitive, and the difficulties of travel were particularly great within central Europe. The industrial revolution was well under way in Britain before any systematic progress took place within the Habsburg realm. Indeed, the collapse of the economy following the Thirty Years' War and the suppression of Protestantism and with it the most vigorous sector of society, had turned much of the monarchy into a backwater.

Life in Germany and Austria was dominated by a rigid social hierarchy, and there was an immense gulf between the nobility and other classes. The aristocracy enjoyed huge economic power, tax concessions, advantages in public life, and preferential treatment and promotion in the army and the church. The highest echelon was that of the princely families such as Esterházy, Schwarzenberg and Lichnowsky. Prince Esterházy (Haydn's patron) owned over ten million acres in Hungary containing some 45,000 households, and had an annual income greater than that of many states. The nobility lived on their country estates in

Court musicians at the festivities for the wedding of Archduke Joseph of Austria and Princess Isabella of Parma, 1760: detail of a painting by Martin van Meytens the younger and his workshop.

the summer, but spent the winter and spring in their palaces in Vienna or Prague. Many of the wealthy aristocrats maintained private orchestras or even theatres, and together with the church were the main employers of musicians and artists. France was the arbiter of taste and culture, and French was the common language of the aristocracy throughout Europe, enabling them to communicate across national barriers.

It would be a mistake, however, to see these scions of the *ancien régime* blithely enjoying their privileged existence until they were swept away by the cataclysm of the French Revolution and subsequent Napoleonic Wars. The eighteenth century saw a growth in the influence of the class of merchants, professional people and civil servants, as manufacture and trade came to rival the traditional sources of wealth. An urban intelligentsia emerged that was receptive to the writings of Enlightenment thinkers. The pervading social system began to be questioned, and ideas concerning the dignity of the individual were already circulating at the time of Mozart's birth through the activities of writers such as Voltaire, Diderot and Rousseau.

Nevertheless, the church continued to be a major force in public life. About two-thirds of the Holy Roman Empire was Protestant, but the political power was almost entirely in the hands of the Catholic states. Even rulers were obliged to comply. For example, Augustus the Strong, the ebullient elector of Saxony who is said to have fathered 354 illegitimate children, ruled a Protestant state from Dresden. But when he became a candidate for the throne of Poland, he converted to Catholicism even though his own subjects objected and his wife left him.

The principality of Salzburg was a small state in European terms. It was an ecclesiastical state ruled by a prince-archbishop elected by the cathedral chapter. The prince-archbishop was not an imperial elector, so had less political influence than the archbishops of Mainz, Cologne or Trier. However, the ruler had the distinction of being the highest-ranking archbishop in the empire, so Salzburg had more prominence than was warranted by its size or economic importance. Protestants were not tolerated, and there was a massive forced exodus of religious refugees to Prussia early in the century.

The prince-archbishop had the same powers and responsibilities in Salzburg as did the autonomous rulers of secular states. He was responsible for the economy and security of the principality, and for the welfare of its inhabitants. There was a court whose members included both senior churchmen and the local nobility, and where worldly display and ceremony could be just as magnificent as in any non-ecclesiastical state. Music was an important element in courtly entertainment and in ceremonial events. Salzburg therefore supported a *Kapelle*, or musical establishment of instrumental players and singers. The Kapelle performed both at the court and the cathedral. It formed the background for Mozart's own musical education and early experience.

CHAPTER 2

Mozart's Family and Birth

The central influence on Mozart's life and development was his father Leopold. Leopold was an active, hard-working man and talented teacher who channelled his ambitions through his children. His astuteness and worldly sophistication allowed him to steer a successful course through the complexities of protocol and etiquette during the family's concert tours through Europe. He believed that his son was a divine miracle, and that his duty was to foster this God-given genius. It is doubtful whether Mozart's creativity would have blossomed and been maintained throughout his life without this intense nurture. The composer

Mozart's father Leopold, painted in about 1765. The portrait is attributed to Pietro Antonio Lorenzoni.

not only acquired his musical education from his father but, until he finally broke free in his late twenties, his entire life was moulded by Leopold's beliefs and attitudes.

Leopold Mozart was not a native of Salzburg, but of the southern German imperial free city of Augsburg. He was born in 1719, the son of a bookbinder. He spent the first eighteen years of his life in Augsburg before moving to Salzburg to enter the Benedictine university as a student of philosophy and law in 1737. After a promising start academically, he began to neglect his studies in favour of music. In 1740 he abandoned the university altogether, and entered the service of a senior canon of the cathedral as musician and valet. Three years later, he was appointed

*An anonymous portrait of
Mozart's mother Maria Anna,
painted in about 1775.*

violinist to the Salzburg court and cathedral, then ruled by the Prince-Archbishop Baron Leopold Firmian. In adult life, Leopold had little to do with his family in Augsburg, who may have been disappointed by his decision not to take holy orders.

Leopold married Maria Anna Pertl in 1747, when he was twenty-eight and she was twenty-six. Maria Anna was the daughter of a senior local administrator in nearby St Gilgen. The couple were considered very handsome, and Leopold Mozart's later letters express great affection for his wife. However, she remained a subordinate character in the family. She was brought up in a society that provided girls with few opportunities for education. She appears to have played little part in major family decisions, but provided quiet support during the extraordinary early lives of Mozart and his sister.

The couple experienced a tragic sequence of births and early deaths of their children over the next seven years. Their first son was born in 1748 but died after six weeks. The second child lived three days, and the third survived only three months. Their fourth child was Maria Anna, born in 1751 and always known as Nannerl within the family. The following year another boy was born who lived for three months, while their sixth child was born in May 1754 but died in late June. Wolfgang was their seventh and last child, and was born on 27 January 1756.

Mozart was christened Joannes Chrysostomus Wolfgangus Theophilus. The first two names come from St John Chrysostom, the fourth-century archbishop of Constantinople whose saint's day falls on 27 January. Wolfgang was the name of his maternal grandfather. Theophilus is Greek for Gottlieb, one of the names of Mozart's godfather Johann Gottlieb Pergmayr, a town councillor and Salzburg merchant. Theophilus also translates into Amadeus, and Mozart began using this version of his name from the time of his first visit to Italy in 1769.

During this period of childbirth and death, Leopold Mozart gradually rose through the ranks of the Salzburg court music or *Hofkapelle.* In 1744 he took responsibility for teaching the violin to the choirboys, and he was promoted to second violinist in the orchestra in 1758. His talents as a teacher culminated in the publication in 1756 of his violin tutor *A Treatise on the Fundamental Principles of Violin Playing* (the *Violinschule*). This primer was reprinted many times and translated into several languages, and became a standard text for several decades. At the same time, he was composing prolifically. Over his early years in Salzburg, he wrote more than twenty-five symphonies, a large number of serenades, twelve oratorios, marches and incidental music. Almost none of this music was ever published, but was kept in manuscript form for use by local musicians.

In 1757, the year after Wolfgang's birth, Leopold wrote a 'Report on the present state of the musical establishment' in Salzburg. This provides an interesting insight into the way music-making was carried out. The court music consisted of about thirty orchestral musicians, including a

Mozart was born in the third-floor apartment of this house (now Getreidegasse 9) in Salzburg.
Here Maria Anna Mozart gave birth to seven children in eight years.

large number of violinists and string players, four bassoonists, three
oboists and flautists, and two horn players. Many of the string players
could double on wind instruments as well. Music-making was under the
supervision of the director or *Kapellmeister*, at that time Johann Ernst
Eberlin, a composer much admired by Leopold and later by Wolfgang.
The vice-Kapellmeister was Giuseppe Lolli, an Italian musician for
whom the Mozarts had little time. There were also three 'court composers', among whom Leopold was numbered. These court composers
together with the Kapellmeister rotated responsibilities for all the music
of the court for a week at a time. During this week, the person acting as

Frontispiece from Leopold Mozart's Violinschule *(published Augsburg 1756) including a portrait engraved by Jakob Andreas Friedrich after Matthias Gottfried Eichler.*

director decided on what should be played, and performed either his own or other people's compositions. The music itself was directed by the leader of the orchestra (or *Konzertmeister*), or from the keyboard by the continuo player, and there was seldom a 'conductor' in the modern sense.

Apart from their duties in the cathedral and at court, the musicians in Salzburg were in regular demand for music-making in private houses, for outdoor serenades, ceremonies, and for events at the university. With a relatively small and captive audience, it was essential that new music was produced for a variety of occasions. Leopold greatly admired speed of composition, and felt that composers ought to be able to write tasteful music in an efficient manner. This view of music-making as a practical rather than spiritual activity, and the sense that the composer should be able to fulfil the particular requirements of the occasion promptly, were feelings that pervaded Mozart's own working life as well.

Despite the fact that the late eighteenth century produced many of the greatest figures of classical music, the status of musicians was relatively humble. At the time of Mozart's birth, the Baroque order was still in place in many parts of Europe, and the position of the artist was fixed on the lower rungs of the social hierarchy. Career options were limited, and even for talented musicians of Leopold's generation there were few alternatives to taking up a post as a servant-musician in an aristocratic household or ecclesiastical court. Such individuals were required to wear uniform and often to carry out other duties in the household. On the other hand, appointment to a court brought with it some security and a modicum of welfare in terms of medical services and care for the retired. Leopold Mozart was reconciled to such a life, and also thought it to be the goal towards which his son Wolfgang should strive. But Wolfgang belonged to a different generation, in which the attitudes of the feudal past were giving way to enlightened belief in self-determination. This fundamental conflict of world views was one of the factors that later led to the estrangement of father and son.

Leopold Mozart's status in Salzburg reached its pinnacle after the death of Eberlin in 1762. By this time, Salzburg was ruled by the generous and music-loving Archbishop Schrattenbach. Leopold applied for the post of Kapellmeister, but that job went to Lolli and he had to be content with becoming vice-Kapellmeister. From that time on, he was continually bypassed for the senior musical position by a series of mediocre Italians. This is perhaps not so surprising when one considers the fact that his musical efforts were now being directed primarily towards the development of his children's abilities.

Almost nothing is known about the first five years of Wolfgang Mozart's life. His sister Nannerl was five years older than him, and was already showing marked talent in her piano lessons with their father. Wolfgang was apparently attracted to playing the keyboard by his third year. Early in 1761, when Mozart was four years old, handwritten notes began to be inserted in Nannerl's music book after certain pieces. Leopold wrote, 'This piece was learned by Wolfgangerl on 24 January 1761, three days before his fifth birthday, between nine and 9.30 in the evening', and two days later, 'This minuet and trio was learned by Wolfgangerl within half an hour on 26 January 1761, a day before his fifth birthday, at about half past nine at night.'

It remains a mystery how he progressed so spectacularly that within a year he was able to perform before the Empress Maria Theresa in Vienna. An exceptional combination of genetic influences on musicality and industriousness almost certainly underpinned his genius. Some insight may also perhaps be gained from considering the early experience of musical prodigies of later eras. For example, the early twentieth-century composer Richard Strauss was born into an intensely musical environment in Munich, where his father was a virtuoso horn player. His parents reacted with enthusiasm to the most trivial indications of musicality in the infant, and his mother proudly recalled how at the age of three he smiled when he heard the sound of the horn. Like Mozart, Strauss began to compose when he was five. Wolfgang's case would have been helped both by his father being a teacher of renown, and by having a model to emulate in his older sister. Another important consideration may be the fact that he was the last of a large number of children, five of whom had died young. Psychologists studying the families of exceptional individuals have noted that this pattern is rather common. The death of older siblings may lead parents to invest particular devotion and attention to the surviving children. Wolfgang, and posterity, may unwittingly have benefited from the sad catalogue of birth and death in the Mozart family.

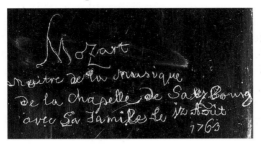

Leopold Mozart scratched his name on this pane of glass when the family visited Frankfurt in 1763.

CHAPTER 3

Travels as a Child Virtuoso

We know very little about the first expedition of the Mozart family out of the narrow confines of Salzburg. In January 1762 they travelled to Munich for a three-week period, during which the five-year-old Wolfgang and his ten-year-old sister performed for the ruler, the Elector Maximilian III. In September they embarked on their first important visit to Vienna, where they were to stay until the end of the year. The capital of the Habsburg kingdom was not in the happiest of states. The Seven Years' War was drawing to a close; although there were no major battles during the 1762 summer campaign, the optimism with which Empress Maria Theresa and her court had entered the conflict had long since dissipated. Nonetheless, for Leopold and his children, the visit was a considerable success.

Many of the details of this, and indeed of the other musical tours of Mozart's childhood, have been preserved mainly through the long and detailed letters from Leopold to their Salzburg landlord Johann Lorenz Hagenauer. Much of the information is factual, although Leopold's

A watercolour of Mozart with his father and sister painted in 1763 in Paris by Louis Carrogis de Carmontelle.

accounts of the reception of his children are undoubtedly coloured by the justifiable pride he felt in them. The letters provide insight into the care with which Leopold prepared for these concert tours. The principal method of earning money was through performing in private to wealthy patrons. Leopold furnished himself with introductions to influential people, and encouraged aristocratic contacts to inform others about the young prodigies, thereby extending the roster of patrons. It is also apparent from these same letters that Leopold expected an intense level of work from his children, even at an early age.

The weather was miserable when the family arrived in Vienna on 6 October, but two days later Wolfgang and Nannerl appeared at a musical soirée at the palace of Count Collalto. They were taken up by the Countess Sinzendorf who used her influence to have them presented on the next day to a Count Wilczek and, more importantly, to Prince Rudolph Colloredo on 11 October. Prince Colloredo was vice-chancellor of the monarchy, and moved in the highest aristocratic circles in Vienna, so the Mozarts rapidly came into contact with the upper echelons of society.

Later in their careers as child musicians, Leopold Mozart worked out a programme of musical feats and demonstrations of Wolfgang and Nannerl's abilities at the keyboard, on the violin, and in singing. It is probable, however, that at this early stage their music-making was confined to the harpsichord. We do not know all of the fees they were able to command, but for a number of appearances they were paid six ducats (or twenty-seven gulden). This was a very substantial sum, and can be put into context by the fact that Leopold Mozart's annual salary as second violinist translated into 295 Viennese gulden. Since the children often performed twice in a day, this means that for two days' work they earned about one-third of Leopold's yearly salary in Salzburg.

Two days after their appearance at Prince Colloredo's, the family were commanded to appear before the imperial household at the magnificent palace of Schonbrünn from three to six o'clock in the afternoon. The seven-year-old Marie Antoinette, the future queen of France, was present together with her parents and other members of the family.

Wolfgang made a great impression. According to Leopold, he jumped up on the empress's lap, put his arms round her neck and kissed her. The success of the visit, however, did not distract Leopold from the main business. That same evening the children appeared at the palace of another aristocrat for a further six ducats.

The schedule of activities on 15 October illustrates this relentless pursuit of celebrity. In the morning, Wolfgang and Nannerl were sent two sets of court clothes by the empress. Wolfgang's suit had originally been made for her son the Archduke Maximilian, a boy of his own age. At 2.30 p.m. they went to one aristocratic household, gave a presentation later in the afternoon at a second palace, and in the evening were guests of Count (later Prince) Kaunitz. Kaunitz was the Empress Maria Theresa's chief adviser, and one of the greatest politicians of the eighteenth century. He was a man of eccentric habits, terrified of illness, hating the open air and refusing to allow windows to be opened, and brushing his teeth and gums in public at the dinner table after he had eaten. The presumably exhausted children stayed at the soirée until 9.0 p.m. Next day there was a similar programme, with a visit to the youngest archdukes at the imperial palace in Vienna (the Hofburg) in the afternoon, and an appearance at the palace of the Hungarian chancellor in the evening.

All this activity was very lucrative. The empress sent 100 ducats (equivalent to 450 gulden), and the nobility made arrangements up to one week in advance to book an appearance. Wolfgang was the special attraction, not only for his musical ability but also because of his unselfconscious childish charm. However, their success was fragile. It depended critically on the health of the children, and later in the month Wolfgang collapsed with a fever and rash, incorrectly diagnosed as scarlet fever. He was incapacitated for two weeks, and Leopold Mozart fulminated at the loss of perhaps fifty ducats. But it could have been much worse. The family was living in cramped quarters above a carpenter's shop in a single large room, Leopold sharing a bed with Wolfgang, and Nannerl with her mother. Infectious disease could strike with distressing rapidity; one of the empress's children, the thirteen-year-old

The young Mozart playing during a reception given by Prince Louis-François de Conti at his residence in the Temple, Paris. Painted in 1766 by Michel Barthélemy Ollivier.

Princess Johanna who had taken Wolfgang's hand and shown him around Schonbrünn Palace, was dead from typhus by the end of the year.

During Wolfgang's illness, the family expenses increased with doctor's fees, so their outlay totalled about one ducat a day. They recouped to a certain extent during the remainder of their stay in Vienna. Leopold, however, had outstayed his leave from his official duties, so on 31 December they set out on the return journey to Salzburg.

This first short visit to Vienna had more than fulfilled Leopold's expectations. The Mozarts' return to Salzburg was greeted with acclaim. They received a particular mark of favour when the Archbishop Count Schrattenbach cancelled the plans for his birthday celebrations in favour of an impromptu concert by the two children. Leopold Mozart's promotion to vice-Kapellmeister was confirmed. He soon began planning a second and much more ambitious tour, deciding that his children's astonishing musicianship should be displayed as widely as possible. This was to take the family away from Salzburg for more than three years, and to have a profound influence on Mozart's musical development.

The Grand Tour:
'Every day God performs fresh miracles through this child'

The family set off from Salzburg on 9 June 1763, and almost at once encountered one of the problems endemic to eighteenth-century travel: the wheel of their carriage broke. The roads in Germany were considered particularly poor in comparison with those of France or England, and tended to deteriorate rapidly with bad weather. Nonetheless, they arrived safely in Munich three days later, and Wolfgang performed at the court of Elector Maximilian the day after. Over the next six months, they travelled slowly north-west through Germany, stopping at Augsburg, Ulm, Schwetzingen, Heidelberg, Mannheim, Mainz and Frankfurt, then on through Coblenz to the Austrian Netherlands. They did not venture further into central Germany or Saxony, even though Frederick the Great's sister tried to persuade them to visit Berlin. The central and eastern areas of Germany were suffering from the devastation of the Seven Years' War, so the prospects of financial success were poor.

At each of the major cities or courts along their route, the family stopped for a few days so that the children could perform. In an era when communication was limited and news did not necessarily travel with speed, Leopold could not expect that the musicians and authorities in German cities and minor courts would have heard of his children. At every stop he therefore acquired letters of introduction to the courts further along their route. As soon as they arrived Leopold would call on his contact to see if a presentation at court or a concert could be arranged. Sometimes they were unsuccessful. They travelled to Ludwigsburg to try to obtain an audience with Duke Carl Eugen of Württemberg, whose Kapellmeister was the celebrated Italian composer Niccolò Jommelli. Leopold called on Jommelli the day after their arrival, but was told by the Italian that the duke was busy hunting and would be likely to keep them waiting for at least two weeks. They therefore moved on within a couple of days.

The title page of Mozart's first published works, 1764.

Leopold soon realized that their tour would not be successful financially if they relied solely on audiences with princes, and playing in the residences of the nobility. He therefore began to organize concerts in inns or public halls. These concerts soon took on the character of sensational events rather than serious musical occasions. The children's exceptional musicianship was not sufficient to attract a large public audience; they had to be seen performing prodigious feats as well. This advertisement for a concert in Frankfurt in August 1763 is an example:

> The girl, who is in her twelfth year, and the boy, who is in his seventh, will not only play at the harpsichord or forte-piano, the former performing the most difficult pieces by the greatest masters; but the boy will also play a concerto on the violin, accompany symphonies on the clavier, completely cover the manual or keyboard of the clavier, and play on the cloth as well as though he had the keyboard under his eyes; he will furthermore accurately name from a distance any note that might be sounded for him either singly or in chords, on the clavier or on every imaginable instrument including bells, glasses and clocks.

It can be seen that Wolfgang was the star of the show. Although Nannerl played the piano with skill and elegance, it was her younger brother who performed on the violin, improvised, or played with the keys covered. Wolfgang's health and well-being were central to the family's fortunes, so even minor illnesses such as catching a cold disrupted their plans. The pressure may have told on the little boy in other ways as well: Leopold relates in a letter dating from August how he found Wolfgang crying in bed one morning because he was missing his friends in Salzburg.

The family arrived in Paris in mid-November, having spent the previous month in Brussels. They lodged with the Bavarian ambassador, and shortly after their arrival, the two children were painted in water-colour along with their father by L. C. de Carmontelle. This picture was soon engraved, and shows Wolfgang as a diminutive creature at the keyboard, bewigged and formally dressed. The contrast between his musical sophistication and childlike innocence appealed in Paris just as it had in Vienna. At the end of the year, they went to Versailles, and on New Year's Day 1764 they were presented to Louis XV and his family. The formal court was soon won over by the charming children, and Wolfgang stood beside the queen throughout dinner, talking to her and eating from her plate.

The family found a new champion in Baron Friedrich Melchior Grimm, a diplomat and author, whose *Correspondance Littéraire* was widely distributed to sovereigns and aristocrats throughout Europe. He was overwhelmed not only by the young Mozart's dexterity but by his musical imagination. On 1 December 1763, he had written that Mozart

> is such an extraordinary phenomenon that one is hard put to it to believe what one sees with one's eyes and hears with one's ears. It means little for this child to perform with the greatest precision the most difficult pieces, with hands that can hardly stretch a sixth: but what is really incredible is to see him improvise for an hour on end and in doing so give rein to the inspiration of his genius and to a mass of enchanting ideas...

This is one of the earliest indications of Mozart's talent extending beyond precocious technical skills into realms of true creativity.

Their five-month stay in Paris was relatively remunerative, and their income would have been even greater if Wolfgang had not fallen ill, possibly with tonsillitis, in February. Leopold also found time to have some of Wolfgang's earliest compositions, a set of sonatas for piano and violin, engraved and published. The sonatas were written out in Leopold's handwriting, and were modelled on the music of Johann Schobert, a popular German composer resident in Paris who died three years later (along with his family and cook) from eating poisonous mushrooms. In April, Leopold told Hagenauer that he was planning to bank 200 louis d'or, a very considerable sum.

London: 'The welcome which we have been given here exceeds all others'

That same month, they decided to travel on to London. They had never seen the sea and were clearly nervous about crossing the English Channel, and Leopold instructed Hagenauer to have eight masses said for them in Salzburg. Fortunately, there was no mishap, and within less than a week the children were performing before King George III and Queen Charlotte at Buckingham Palace. This astonishing progress is another mark of the extraordinary interest that surrounded the prodigies.

Soon after arriving, they met the English musician Charles Burney, who travelled widely through Europe and published important records of the state of music-making in different countries. Burney thoroughly examined the boy, observing him playing at sight, filling in harmonies and accompaniments, and imitating various dramatic styles. He was amazed and described Wolfgang's abilities with enthusiasm. He touchingly adds that when the tests were over, Wolfgang 'played at marbles, in the true childish way of one who knows nothing'.

Their stay in London was to continue for over a year, more by accident than design. The main reason was that Leopold fell ill in the summer of 1764 and took several weeks to recover. His illness had unexpected benefits in bringing Wolfgang into contact for an extended period with several of the leading composers of the day. The most important was Johann Christian Bach, the youngest and most famous son of J. S. Bach. Bach had come to London in 1762 and was based in England for the last twenty years of his short life. His vast

No. 180 Ebury Street where the Mozart family stayed during their London visit.

output included operas, symphonies, concertos and keyboard music. With Carl Friedrich Abel, he established the celebrated Bach–Abel concerts, held at Carlisle House in Soho Square. The first series took place in the spring of 1765 when the Mozarts were still in London, and attracted leading virtuosi from the whole of Europe.

Wolfgang endeared himself to Bach and learned greatly from him. In her old age, Nannerl reminisced about an occasion when Bach held the boy between his knees, and the two alternated playing through a complete sonata with such synchrony and understanding that it was impossible to tell who was playing at any one moment. Wolfgang was strongly influenced by Bach's style, and his early symphonies and piano works were modelled on Bach's compositions. Bach was active at the Italian opera in London, and it is probable that this first attracted Mozart to the genre. In addition to Bach, the boy heard the music of symphonists such as Thomas Arne, William Boyce and Carl Abel. Indeed, he copied out one of Abel's symphonies which was later mistakenly published as one of his own.

Mozart's first attempt to write a symphony himself probably came in the summer of 1764 when he was eight years old. The family had been advised to seek fresh air outside London in order to help Leopold's recovery, and they moved to Chelsea. According to his sister, Mozart composed his first symphony in order to occupy himself, and he wanted to use all the instruments of the orchestra, especially the trumpets and kettledrums. 'I had to copy it out as I sat at his side. Whilst he composed and I copied he said to me: Remind me to give the horns something worthwhile to do!' This symphony may not have survived, since his first known symphony (K16 in E flat major) dates from the autumn of 1764 and shows strong resemblance to the works of London contemporaries. He seems to have composed a considerable amount of orchestral work over these months, for when advertisements appeared for a concert in February 1765, it was stated that all the 'overtures' would be by the young Wolfgang.

Leopold Mozart vigorously continued his campaign to maximize popular interest in his children, and was not even above using small deceptions. When the family arrived in London in April 1764, Wolfgang was eight years old; but in all public announcements advertising their activities, Leopold took one year off his son's age. Throughout 1764, Wolfgang was described as being seven years old, eight during 1765, and so on for the remainder of their European tour.

This falsehood about his age was probably a device to encourage audiences that would not have attended for musical reasons alone. Although London was a major musical centre, Leopold could not rely on aristocratic patronage to recoup the costs associated with his illness, and resorted to more public arenas. From March 1765, notices began to appear in the *Public Advertiser*, inviting the public to the Mozarts' lodgings any afternoon between twelve and three to test the children's musical skills at five shillings per person. By July 1765 they were desperate to leave England, and the children were reduced to playing in the afternoons in the upper rooms of a tavern in the City for an entry fee of two shillings and six pence (about $1\frac{1}{4}$ gulden).

They finally set sail in August, shortly after Leopold had presented Wolfgang's engraved sonatas to the British Museum. The next six months were spent in Holland (then the independent United Provinces), mainly in Amsterdam and The Hague. Compared with other places on the tour, Holland was something of a musical backwater. This, however, was to their advantage, since there was little competition from other entertainments. Wolfgang had time to compose six more sonatas for piano and violin (K26–31). This combination was very popular among amateur musicians, and it was assumed that the keyboard would be played by a lady with a gentleman performing the less demanding accompanying violin part. They gave three concerts at The Hague in September 1765, and several in Leiden, Amsterdam and Utrecht. But once again their plans were disrupted. Nannerl fell seriously ill in September, probably with typhoid fever. She was so ill that she received extreme unction, and it was three months before she recovered fully. No sooner had she begun to recuperate than Wolfgang fell ill. Leopold describes how in four weeks the illness 'has made him so wretched that he is not only absolutely unrecognizable, but has nothing left but his tender skin and his little bones and for the last five days has been carried daily from his bed to a chair'.

They only began to perform in public again at the end of January 1766. Leopold had planned to stay in the Low Countries for a couple of months before returning to Salzburg by way of Paris. In fact, they reached Paris in May 1766, and after two months began their return journey by way of Dijon, Lyons, Geneva, Lausanne and Zürich. They had hoped to visit Voltaire while in Geneva, but the writer was unwell. By November they were back in Munich, where Wolfgang again played for Elector Maximilian, and they finally reached Salzburg at the end of the month.

Wolfgang's performances had astonished connoisseurs, rulers and general audiences alike. When he returned to Salzburg, acquaintances noticed an added maturity in comparison with the earlier years. By any criteria, the child's life was extraordinary. Between the ages of seven and eleven, Mozart had spent most of his time in foreign countries with unfamiliar languages, and probably never stayed even a day out of sight of his parents or sister. He did not attend school or have any formal education, and it is not known whether he had more than passing contact with children of his own age. Leopold had personally ensured that his children learned languages, mathematics and other subjects, and exerted firm discipline over his family. There are no signs that the children ever disobeyed his wishes. In a telling letter to Hagenauer shortly before they returned to Salzburg, Leopold fretted about the arrangements that were being put in train for the family to move house in the city. His greatest concern was with the loss of time and disruption that might be caused by the move:

> Every moment I lose is lost forever. And if I ever guessed how precious for youth is time, I realize it now. You know that my children are accustomed to work. But if with the excuse that one thing prevents another they were to accustom themselves to hours of idleness, my whole plan would crumble to pieces. Habit is an iron shirt.

Yet Mozart emerged as a likeable, engaging child, as enthusiastic for music as ever. He took advantage of the unparalleled musical experience of his early years in fashioning his mature compositional style. He does not appear to have been overwhelmed by the dizzying social success of the tour. It says much for the stability of his character, and for the firm support of his down-to-earth family, that he survived this extraordinary childhood relatively unscathed.

Part of the programme for a concert given by the Accademia Filarmonica of Mantua in Mozart's honour in 1770.

CHAPTER 4
Mozart's Journeys as an Adolescent: Vienna and Italy

The Mozart family spent the first eight months of 1767 back in Salzburg where Leopold resumed his duties at the cathedral and court. Joseph Haydn's brother Michael had been appointed to the musical establishment back in 1763, but this was the first period during which the Mozarts had any contact with him. Michael Haydn was a prolific composer of both sacred and secular music, and it was inevitable that his style had some influence on Mozart's early church music. The two collaborated on a cantata or sacred *Singspiel* which was performed in March 1767, and during these months Mozart also adapted sonatas by German composers resident in Paris into four piano 'concertos' (K37, 39, 40 and 41). These were presumably intended for his own concerts, and contain little original music.

On 11 September 1767, the family set out once more on a journey that was to keep them away until January 1769. They were bound for Vienna, probably to participate in the celebrations surrounding the wedding of Empress Maria Theresa's daughter, the Archduchess Maria Josepha, to King Ferdinand of Naples. They took lodgings in the house of a goldsmith, but their plans were soon plunged into chaos. There was an outbreak of smallpox in the city, and the archduchess was one of the early victims. Worse still, the children of the goldsmith caught the disease. Leopold Mozart moved out of the house immediately with Wolfgang, leaving his wife and daughter until suitable arrangements could be made. It was an interesting response to the crisis that emphasized once again Leopold's priorities and devotion to his son. They all fled from Vienna to Brno and thence to Olomouc (Olmütz), deep in Moravia. But it was too late, since Wolfgang caught the illness which was to incapacitate him for several weeks. It left a permanent mark on his appearance, and his

View of Vienna from the Upper Belvedere, the Baroque palace built for Prince Eugene of Savoy. Painted by Bernardo Bellotto in 1759/61.

sister Nannerl later recalled him being a handsome child before being disfigured by the pox.

Wolfgang had recovered sufficiently to return to Vienna with his family in January 1768. They were received by the imperial family at court, where not only Maria Theresa but also her son the Emperor Joseph II showed them great favour. They remained in the city for the carnival season and Lent, but were evidently not as successful as before. Prince Kaunitz would not receive them on account of Wolfgang's smallpox, and expenses mounted. The archbishop in Salzburg decreed that Leopold was no longer to be paid if he did not return to his post in April. Nevertheless, they remained in Vienna, and the reason was that Leopold had decided that his son should write an opera.

An Italian stage-coach c. 1775.

This opera project should have marked a new phase in Mozart's development, and a transition from youthful performer to membership of an adult musical world where he would begin to be compared with mature composers, and compete with them for commissions. But in encouraging the plan, Leopold Mozart misjudged the situation, assuming that fellow professionals would be enthusiastic about his son's precocious talent. The opera, *La finta semplice*, was a comic opera or *opera buffa*, and production and payment became irretrievably bogged down by intrigue within the Viennese musical establishment. The opera was the responsibility of an Italian impresario Giuseppe Affligio (or Afflisio). Affligio, variously known as Don Pepe il Cadetto and Maratti, was a colourful gambler and entrepreneur, and the finances of the theatre were fragile. It is perhaps not surprising that he did not go out of his way to promote the work of a twelve-year-old with no experience of opera buffa, and probably rather limited command of Italian. Leopold's efforts culminated in a bitter petition to the emperor, which probably served to alienate the hitherto supportive Habsburgs. Nonetheless, he remained unrepentant about his efforts to promote his son:

> Should I perhaps sit down in Salzburg with the empty hope of some better fortune, let Wolfgang grow up, and allow myself and my children to be made fools of until I reach the age which prevents me from travelling and until he attains the age and physical appearance which no longer attract admiration for his merits?

Another less prestigious opera venture did come to fruition, namely the Singspiel *Bastien und Bastienne*. It is thought to have been commissioned by the celebrated physician and champion of hypnotic therapies, Anton Mesmer. Dr Mesmer had married a rich widow of noble descent who lived in a mansion in the Landstrasse suburb of Vienna, and it is here that this short but charming opera is supposed to have received its première in the autumn. The long sojourn in Vienna was beneficial to Mozart in other ways as well, for he heard a great deal of modern music, including orchestral works by composers such as Dittersdorf, Haydn and Vanhal. He learned new styles from these musicians, and in particular to use the orchestral wind more imaginatively than did his London models. He responded by composing several symphonies that show a growing maturity.

The four members of the Mozart family returned to their old apartment in Lorenz Hagenauer's house in Salzburg in January 1769. They were never to travel together again, and for most of the next year they stayed in the city. Mozart was beginning to make an impression on the musical establishment, composing several masses and an important set of multiple-movement 'cassations' or serenades (K63, 99 and 100). Leopold was busy preparing a new edition of his *Violinschule*, but in addition he was planning the next ambitious journey, this time to Italy.

Italy: 'My heart is completely enchanted with all these pleasures, because it is so jolly on this journey'

Throughout the eighteenth century, a period of work and study in Italy was seen as essential for aspiring German composers. Leopold must have felt that contact with Italian music would complete his son's education,

Portrait of the fourteen-year-old Mozart painted in Verona by Saverio dalla Rosa in 1770.

Thomas Linley the younger painted by Thomas Gainsborough (1727–88).

and fit him for his new role as a young professional composer. Father and son set out in December 1769, heading first for Verona, where Mozart gave two concerts and they heard operas by Johann Hasse and the Italian Pietro Guglielmi. They then moved on to Milan, one of the cultural centres of Italy and the capital of the Austrian province of Lombardy. Here they made contact with Niccolò Piccinni, the doyen of Italian opera composers, and with Giovanni Sammartini, the leading composer of church music in Milan. They were taken up by Count Firmian, governor-general of Lombardy, and a man of great taste and intellect. Count Firmian presented the young Mozart with a complete edition of the works of Metastasio, the poet whose libretti dominated eighteenth-century *opera seria*. A grand concert was held at Firmian's palace on 12 March 1770, for which Mozart composed several arias to words by Metastasio. Better still, Firmian was instrumental in securing for Mozart the commission to write an opera for the next winter season in Milan.

They moved on to Bologna in March. Count Firmian had given them a letter of introduction to the elderly Field Marshal Count Pallavicini, who was to prove a valuable friend later in the summer. The next stop was Florence, capital of the duchy of Tuscany and ruled by Joseph II's brother Leopold (known to the Italians as Pietro Leopoldo). Mozart was received at the Pitti Palace on 1 April, and was subjected to the type of musical examination that was so common in his early years, being tested with difficult sightreading, fugues to complete and themes to improvise. His father later informed the family back in Salzburg that these were 'played off and worked out as easily as one eats a piece of bread'. They did not stay long in Florence, because they wished to reach Rome for Holy Week. However, Mozart did have time to meet Thomas Linley, a young English composer then studying in Florence. The two boys were the same age, and took an instant liking to one another. Years later, Mozart was to remember Linley, who died tragically in a boating accident when only twenty-two, with warmth and affection.

When they reached Rome, they were able to present no fewer than twenty letters of introduction from Count Firmian, Count Pallavicini and others to the aristocracy and leading ecclesiastical figures of the city. On 11 April they attended a service in the Sistine Chapel. The famous *Miserere* by the seventeenth-century composer Gregorio Allegri was sung every year during Holy Week in the chapel, but the music and ornamentation were kept a carefully guarded secret in the Vatican. Mozart wrote the piece out from memory after hearing it once or twice, an astonishing feat. They remained in Rome for a month, performing at the palaces of the nobility and being introduced to notables such as Charles Stuart (the Young Pretender), and the wealthy English eccentric William Beckford.

Mozart was beginning to absorb the musical styles with which he had come in contact. The most immediate result was a series of symphonies that are Italianate in style and form (K74, 81, 84 and 97). Throughout the journey, he appears to have been in excellent spirits; Leopold describes him as being 'cheerful and gay and jolly'. Leopold's long letters home to Salzburg were frequently supplemented by short postscripts from his son to Nannerl. These are very affectionate in tone, and discuss the music and performances they have heard, new games he has learned in Italy, and other trivia. He also had some wry observations to make of the people he met. While in Bologna, for example, he made the acquaintance of a Dominican who was famed for his piety:

> For my part I do not believe it, for at breakfast he often takes a cup of chocolate and immediately afterwards a good glass of strong Spanish wine; and I myself have had the honour of lunching with this saint who at table drank a whole decanter and finished up with a full glass of strong wine, two large slices of melon, some peaches, pears, five cups of coffee, a whole plate of birds and two full saucers of milk and lemon. He may, of course, be following some sort of diet, but I do not think so ...

They moved on to Naples in May 1770, where they made the acquaintance of the cultivated British ambassador Sir William Hamilton

A musical chamber group playing in Lord Fortrose's Naples palace, painted by Pietro Fabris in 1770.
It was in settings like this that Mozart played on his Italian tour.

(later the husband of Nelson's mistress, Emma), and came into contact
once again with the composer Niccolò Jommelli. Their main purpose
was to perform at court to King Ferdinand. Following the sudden death
of the Archduchess Josepha in 1767, Ferdinand had married another of
Empress Maria Theresa's daughters, and she now ruled as Queen Maria
Carolina. It is difficult to know which of the sisters was better off.
Ferdinand was an illiterate boor of little taste, superstitious and credulous
in the extreme. His main entertainments appear to have been hunting,
pinching the bottoms of ladies of his court, and playing games with his
attendants. The Mozarts waited in vain to be presented, and over the
weeks their expenses rose. For example, they had to buy new lightweight

suits for the summer; Wolfgang's was made of rose-coloured silk moiré trimmed with silver lace and lined with silk, while Leopold's was of cinnamon-coloured piqué lined with green silk. However, they were fêted by the nobility of Naples, and enjoyed an agreeable month riding in carriages, visiting country estates, and inspecting the newly discovered ruins of Pompeii and Herculaneum. Leopold's confidence in his son's ability was further bolstered by an offer to write an opera for the San Carlo theatre in Naples. Unfortunately this had to be refused, since the commission for Milan had already been settled.

They left Naples in late June, travelling hurriedly to Rome in just over twenty-four hours instead of taking four days for the journey. The reason for their haste is unclear, and it resulted in an injury to Leopold's leg when their carriage overturned. It may be because they had been informed that Pope Clement XIV had decided to confer the title of 'Knight of the Golden Order' (Golden Spur) on the fourteen-year-old composer. An audience with the pope followed before they returned north to Bologna. Here they remained from July to the beginning of October, probably because Leopold's leg injury had still not mended sufficiently for further travel. They spent several weeks at the country estate of Count Pallavicini where they lived in great luxury. They had rooms in the cooler lower floors of the mansion, and were allotted a valet and footman to wait on them. Mozart also had an opportunity to learn from Padre Martini, a Franciscan monk and renowned musical scholar and teacher.

While they were in Bologna, the libretto of the opera for Milan arrived. This was *Mitridate, rè di Ponto*, an adaptation and translation of Racine's tragedy *Mithridate*. This opera was the most important experience of Mozart's first Italian journey, and taught him professionalism in composition. One might expect that he would start writing the music straight away, but this was only partly true. No composers of that era would begin to write arias until they had heard the particular singers who would be involved, and had become familiar with their strengths and vocal preferences. Singers in the eighteenth century had an extraordinary influence over how parts were realized, and were able to veto arias or even have replacements prepared by alternative composers. Mozart therefore had to wait until the *prima donna* reached Milan in early November and the *primo uomo* (castrato) arrived at the beginning of December before he could write their music. Since the première was on 26 December 1770, he had to work extremely rapidly to complete the opera on time. He learned through bitter experience that singers were not easily pleased. Several arias had to be rewritten, and more than ten rejected fragments have survived. Nonetheless, the opening night went well, even though the performance lasted six hours. The opera was given in the Ducal Theatre, which burned down six years later, to be replaced by La Scala. Mozart had a new suit of scarlet silk trimmed with gold and lined with blue satin, and directed the first three nights from the keyboard. *Mitridate* was a spectacular achievement for such a young composer. It was given twenty-two times, and on the strength of its success he was awarded the commission to write the prestigious first opera seria for the 1772–3 carnival season. They therefore left the city well satisfied, passing slowly by way of Verona and Venice back to Salzburg.

Second and third Italian journeys

They were not to remain in Salzburg for long, since before leaving Italy, Mozart had been commissioned to write a work to celebrate the marriage of the Archduke Ferdinand to Maria d'Este of Modena in Milan in the autumn. This commission, which was probably again secured through Count Firmian, resulted in *Ascanio in Alba*, and they set out again in August 1771. Mozart's second journey to Italy must have filled him with high hopes for more permanent employment. The commission for *Ascanio* ostensibly came from the bridegroom's mother, the Empress Maria Theresa, but it was the Archduke Ferdinand himself who had suggested to her that they employ Wolfgang. Unbeknown to the Mozarts, the empress had given a very cool response:

> You ask me to take the young Salzburger into your service ... I do not know why, not believing that you have need of a composer or of useless people ... If however it would give you pleasure, I have no wish to hinder you ... What I say is intended only to prevent your burdening yourself with

The interior of the Ducal Theatre in Milan, laid out for a ball rather than opera. Mitridate *was presented here at the end of 1770. Engraving by Marc Antonio dal Rè.*

useless people ... If they are in your service it degrades that service when these people go about the world like beggars ...

Ascanio was a serenade or masque rather than an opera, with little dramatic structure. It was shown in tandem with an opera seria by Hasse, who had been a favourite composer of European royalty for forty years. The Mozarts had close contact with Hasse during this period, and the old composer formed an interesting opinion of Wolfgang which was critical of Leopold's missionary zeal:

> Young Mozart is certainly marvellous for his age, and I do love him infinitely. The father ... is equally discontented everywhere ... He idolizes his son a little too much, and thus does all he can to spoil him; but I have such a high opinion of the boy's natural good sense that I hope he will not be spoilt in spite of the father's adulation ...

Mozart was provided with lodgings in Milan, sandwiched between violinists upstairs and downstairs, a singing master next door and an oboist opposite. This did not stop him working (indeed he said it gave him plenty of ideas), and *Ascanio* appears to have been favourably received. However, apart from the opera there was little activity in Milan since it was out of season, so they returned to Salzburg in December 1771.

The day after they reached Salzburg, an event occurred that had serious consequences. The elderly archbishop died, and he was replaced after much scheming and lobbying by Hieronymus Colloredo. Colloredo was the son of the Austrian vice-chancellor, and his election represented a diplomatic coup for Emperor Joseph II. Schrattenbach had left the treasury seriously depleted, and Colloredo did much to restore the fortunes of the principality. Colloredo was a member of the enlightened modernizing wing of the church, and approved Joseph's efforts to reduce unnecessary pomp and ceremony. This indirect threat to the musical establishment, coupled with Colloredo's autocratic manner which alienated many Salzburg citizens, later exacerbated Mozart's loathing of the city. Initially, however, father and son may have greeted Colloredo's appointment with some pleasure. The new archbishop was an enthusiastic musician and often joined the professional orchestra with his violin.

Mozart composed the rather pedestrian *Il sogno di Scipione* for the archbishop's installation. The first half of 1772 was a prolific period of composition, with dance music, three divertimento-like string quartets and the Piano Sonata for four hands in D major (K381). Most important was a series of seven symphonies that show distinct advances over earlier works, most particularly in the brilliant Symphony in D major (K133) and more introspective A major (K134).

Mozart and his father seemed delighted to set off for Italy again in late October to fulfil the opera commission for Milan that was to result in *Lucio Silla*. This opera is probably the finest of the grand Italian works, containing a number of very effective dramatic moments. Unfortunately, the production was beset with problems, and the première began three hours late since Archduke Ferdinand was delayed. Although the work was given several times, it appears not to have built on the success of *Mitridate*, and no further commissions followed. Nevertheless, they lingered in Milan for a further three months. Their hopes were now focused on Florence, and on the possibility of being taken into the service of Duke Leopold of Tuscany. Mozart's father feigned a rheumatic illness to prevent them having to return to Salzburg. Mozart himself spent the time in Milan fruitfully, and his first serious efforts at writing string quartets emanate from this period, with a series of six works (K155–60). The delightful motet *Exsultate, jubilate* (K165) with its glittering Alleluia finale was sung by the leading castrato in January 1773, and they attended a new opera by the rising star among Italian composers, Giovanni Paisiello. But they waited in vain for a summons to Florence, and left Italy for the last time in March 1773.

   This journey represented the Mozarts' last effort to obtain employment outside Austria and south Germany. Although the Italians were willing to praise the young musician, their rulers were not prepared to take him into service. Mozart had made an impressive start in writing for the stage, but still had much to learn before perfecting his craft. As a musical experience, the years in Italy were invaluable in making him familiar with the work and style of the leading contemporary composers. This in turn helped to stimulate the maturing of his own creativity over the next few years.

Venanzio Rauzzini, the leading castrato in Mozart's opera Lucio Silla. *Engraving after Hutchisson.*

CHAPTER 5

Interlude: Growing up in Salzburg 1773–7

The years between Mozart's last journey to Italy in 1773 and his departure from Salzburg in late 1777 on the long tour to Mannheim and Paris form an enigmatic interlude. Over this period, he grew from the age of seventeen to twenty-one. For such a precocious youth, one might imagine this to have been a time of youthful exuberance, romance and discovery. But the sketchy information that survives about him confronts us with a paradox. These were years of immense creativity, when Mozart composed with a facility that he was seldom to achieve later in life, and the first masterpieces to establish an enduring place in the repertoire date from this period. Emotionally, by contrast, he appears to have been frozen in adolescent dependence.

Soon after Mozart and his father returned from Italy in March 1773, the family moved from their long-established lodgings with the Hagenauers, taking up residence in the first-floor rooms of the 'Dancing Master's House'. This house is on the Markart-Platz (then the Hannibal-Platz) on the north bank of the river, and the apartment consisted of eight rooms including a large chamber in which concerts and even balls

The large chamber in the Dancing Master's House in which the Mozarts played music and held concerts.

could be held. It was a sign of their growing prosperity that they could afford such substantial accommodation. They settled into Salzburg musical life once again and, over the next three months, Mozart wrote four symphonies. But it was not long before father and son took advantage of the archbishop's absence from Salzburg during the summer to visit Vienna. They stayed in the capital for two months. We do not know the reason for this visit, and certainly at this time of year Mozart was unlikely to have been able to earn much through performances to the nobility. They did, however, have an audience with the empress on 5 August, and it is possible that Leopold had formed yet more plans concerning an appointment for his son in the royal household. Predictably, Mozart again benefited musically from being able to hear the latest compositions in the capital. On this occasion, Joseph Haydn had recently completed his set of six string quartets (op. 20) known as the 'Sun Quartets'. These quartets represent a landmark in classical music, and the transformation of the quartet from a type of light diversion into a serious genre. Mozart was inspired to produce a set of six quartets himself (K168–73). He completed them in the astonishingly short period of less than two months.

Back in Salzburg, Mozart was now Konzertmeister, or leader of the orchestra, a post he shared with Michael Haydn. His compositional output was extraordinary over the next twelve months. He wrote his first string quintet in late 1774, together with his first original piano concerto (K175). Although an early work, he was to perform this concerto successfully in Vienna a decade later, where it became a great favourite. The Bassoon Concerto and the Concertone for two Violins (K190) followed soon after, together with two masses, other church music and several dances written for the carnival season. Perhaps the most important pieces are the five symphonies that date from late 1773 and 1774. Two of these stand out as among his greatest and most startling works – the G minor Symphony (K183) and the Symphony in A major (K201) [CD 1]. Indeed, many commentators date Mozart's development into a great composer from these two works.

He must have been stimulated to write these large-scale works not

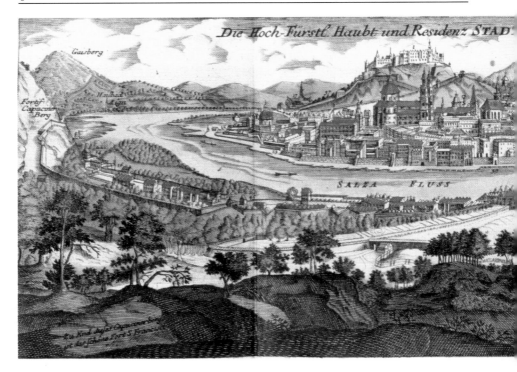

only by the music he had heard in Vienna and Italy, but also by the availability of the Salzburg orchestra. The full extent of his symphonic activity is actually hard to gauge. Nearly one hundred symphonies have been attributed to him by various authorities, but the American scholar Neil Zaslow judges that fewer than sixty are genuine, and some of these are lost. The Kapellmeister was now Domenico Fischietti, who had an established reputation in Europe. The English musician Charles Burney wrote about the Salzburg musical establishment when describing musical activity in Germany, and was enthusiastic about arrangements there:

> The Archbishop and sovereign of Salzburg is very magnificent in his support of music, having usually near a hundred performers, vocal and instrumental,

A panorama of Salzburg around 1745, showing the main city including the cathedral and archbishop's residence on the south bank of the river.

in his service. This Prince is himself a dilettante, and good performer on the violin. He has lately been at great pains to reform his band, which has been accused of being more remarkable for coarseness and noise than delicacy and high-finishing.

This certainly suggests that with the substitution of Fischietti for the ineffective Kapellmeister Lolli, the enthusiasm of the archbishop, and perhaps with the presence of Mozart and Michael Haydn, the strength and vitality of the Salzburg orchestra were greatly enhanced.

However, Mozart still felt constrained by the limitations of the small court and city. His next opportunity for travel was in late 1774 when he was commissioned to write an opera for Munich. This was *La finta giardiniera*, an opera buffa written to a libretto that had been set by an Italian composer for the Rome opera just a few months earlier. He and his father Leopold arrived in Munich on 7 December, and on this occasion were joined by Nannerl in time for the première. Mozart was delighted to be away from Salzburg, as he told his mother in a letter that also describes the reception of the opera. He says that *La finta giardiniera*

> was such a success that it is impossible for me to describe the applause to Mamma. In the first place, the whole theatre was so packed that a great many people were turned away. Then after each aria there was a terrific noise, clapping of hands and cries of 'Viva Maestro'. Her Highness the Electress and the Dowager Electress (who were sitting opposite me) also called out 'Bravo' to me ... I fear that we cannot return to Salzburg very soon and Mamma must not wish it, for she knows how much good it is doing me to be able to breathe freely.

Although it is rarely performed now, this was the first of Mozart's operas to be widely seen in his own time. A German translation was soon made, and presented in Augsburg, Frankfurt and other cities over the next decade.

Despite having to work on the opera, Mozart still found time to compose his first six piano sonatas (K279–84). It appears strange that he had played for so long as a keyboard virtuoso before writing solo sonatas for his own use, but he had already composed sets of brilliant variations to show off his technique. These early sonatas are frequently dismissed as slight works, but they are nonetheless satisfying pieces with subtleties that repay attention.

Little is known about Mozart's emotional relationships over these years. Biographers used to be excited by the series of comments the eighteen-year-old composer made about 'Fräulein Mitzerl' in letters from Munich to his sister: 'Please give all sorts of messages to Jungfrau Mitzerl, and tell her that she must never doubt my love. I see her constantly before me in her ravishing negligée. I have seen many pretty girls here, but have not yet found such a beauty.' In fact, these lighthearted compliments were directed at the sixty-four-year-old Maria Raab, their close neighbour and the owner of the house in which the Mozarts lived.

His return to Salzburg in early March was soon followed by an instruction from the archbishop to compose *Il rè pastore* for a visit to the city by the Archduke Maximilian. Maximilian was the youngest of Maria Theresa's children, and was the same prince whose suit of clothes Mozart had inherited as a six-year-old in Vienna. This opera has exceptional qualities that are too little known, and is sometimes described as a serenata since it may have been performed as a concert piece. Four of his five violin concertos also date from 1775. These show a marked progression as he became more familiar with the genre, and may have been written for the composer himself to perform. More church music was produced, along with a group of arias that were probably written for insertion into operas by other composers. A theatre was opened in the square opposite Mozart's apartment during 1775, and the family regularly attended plays there. Curiously, however, Mozart does not appear to have written much music for it, despite his passion for the stage. His only involvement with the theatre over this period was the provision of incidental music to the play *Thamos, König in Ägypten*, performed by a visiting company in 1776 and 1779.

The opening scene of Il rè pastore. *Engraving from the* Opere *of Pietro Metastasio, 1758. Metastasio's libretto was set more than twenty times in the eighteenth century, and Mozart's version was presented in Salzburg in 1775.*

One reason for Mozart's dislike of Salzburg was his contempt for the behaviour of the musicians. His childhood experience had involved social contact with sophisticated patrons and cultivated people rather than professional musicians, and he resented being seen as one of their number. He was later to compare the Salzburg musicians unfavourably with the players in the Mannheim orchestra:

> That is one of my chief reasons for detesting Salzburg – those coarse, slovenly, dissolute court musicians. Why, no honest man, of good breeding, could possibly live with them! Indeed, instead of wanting to associate with them, he would feel ashamed of them. It is probably for this very reason that musicians are neither popular nor respected among us. Ah, if only the orchestra were organized as they are at Mannheim ... There everything is done seriously. They have good manners, are well dressed, do not go into public houses and swill.

Antonio Brunetti, the solo violinist who joined the establishment in 1776, was the type of musician of whom Mozart disapproved. He was a gambler, and lived with the daughter of the cathedral organist, with whom he had an illegitimate child. Mozart knew full well that musicians and actors tended to be viewed with suspicion by respectable citizens even without this kind of dissolute behaviour. So instead of fraternizing with musicians, the family's social world revolved around a cadre of senior court officials, Salzburg dignitaries and their families. They were friends of the Gilowsky family (court surgeon), the von Mölks (court chancellor), the Barisini family (physicians), Robinigs (factory owners), Haffners (a family of merchants) and the Abbé Bullinger, a former Jesuit. Their friend Joachim von Schiedenhofen was a wealthy Salzburg councillor, with a country estate in Bavaria. His diaries provide much of the scanty information that survives about day-to-day life over these years. There were regular dinners and music-making within this circle, and more frivolous activities too. In 1776, for example, they all attended an assembly during the carnival season in costume, dancing until four or five o'clock in the morning. Schiedenhofen was dressed as a lackey, Leopold Mozart as a porter and Wolfgang as a hairdresser's boy, and other notables as Moors and peasant girls.

Mozart spent 1776 in Salzburg without travelling. The important works

Count Hieronymus Colloredo, Prince-Archbishop of Salzburg 1772–1803. Painting by Franz Xaver König, 1772.

from this year include the 'Haffner' Serenade (K250), the first Lodron divertimento (K247) and the *Serenata notturna* (K239). Two piano concertos were written early in the year along with the Triple Concerto (K242). He also wrote five divertimenti for six wind instruments in 1775 and 1776. These were probably intended for the entertainment of the archbishop, and are amiable works moving far beyond contemporary models in their exploitation of the instruments. There continued to be a steady stream of religious music, but the next significant work was the E flat Piano Concerto (K271) completed in January 1777. From its arresting and original opening to the exhilarating virtuoso finale with its graceful minuet interlude, this is a work of great power and harmonic richness.

Yet despite these masterpieces, Mozart began to suffer from a lack of musical stimulation by 1777. He thrived in a competitive world where he could be excited by other composers' works. Far from being a timeless genius creating in isolation and satisfied with his own internal musical world, he needed a steady infusion of new musical experience to trigger his creativity, and varied opportunities to exercise his skills. His ambitions extended far beyond writing church music and serenades for the local nobility, and the atmosphere in Salzburg was stultifying. He wrote no symphonies after 1775, despite the availability of a good orchestra. After composing the six string quartets in Vienna in 1773, he wrote no more quartets for the next nine years. There were no further piano sonatas, no violin sonatas, and of course no operas. So in March 1777, Leopold submitted a petition to the archbishop requesting that they be allowed to travel once again. Prince Colloredo refused, but later in the year they tried a new tactic, presenting a petition in Wolfgang's own name, asking for him to be released from service. This petition plainly infuriated the archbishop who responded by dismissing both father and son from his service. Leopold was distraught and fell ill. A compromise was reached and it was agreed that Wolfgang could travel in the company of his mother, while Leopold and Nannerl remained in Salzburg. Thus at the age of twenty-one, Mozart was at last able to take his first steps towards independence.

CHAPTER 6

Journey of Discovery: Mannheim and Paris

Mozart's fifteen-month tour to Mannheim and Paris was not a musical triumph. He composed comparatively few major works, and his only important commission was for the 'Paris' Symphony in June 1778. He also failed in the main purposes of the journey, which were to make money, and to secure a permanent post as Kapellmeister at a court outside Salzburg. On the other hand, the journey was a key rite of passage in his personal life. He experienced the exhilaration and disappointments of love, great sorrow with the unexpected death of his mother, and a transformation in his relationship with his father. He also came to understand more about his position in society. Until this tour, he probably did not realize that his early success and protection from the rigid social hierarchies of the era owed as much to his childish charm, the proper behaviour of his family, and the entrepreneurial skills of his father, as to his own talent.

Maximilian III of Bavaria with his wife and sister, painted by J. N. Grooth in 1758.

Munich and Augsburg

Wolfgang and his mother Maria Anna left Salzburg on 23 September 1777 in high spirits. He wrote to his father that evening describing various incidents on the road and expressing delight at finally escaping from the archbishop's service. Leopold responded with a letter that was guaranteed to depress them, explaining how he had prayed and lay in bed as if in mourning, how Nannerl wept so much that she ended up vomiting, and how even their dog Bimperl was disconsolate. This exchange was to set the tone for their correspondence over the next months, for whenever Wolfgang wrote with enthusiasm about his plans, or pleasure in the people and places he encountered, Leopold responded with gloomy descriptions of his own situation, and stern reminders that the family's future rested on the young man's shoulders.

Mozart's first hope when he arrived in Munich was that the ruler, Elector Maximilian of Bavaria, would take him into service. He immediately learned a lesson about the real world of professional musicians. In his youth, the aristocracy had competed to have him perform at their

*Maria Anna Thekla Mozart,
known in the family as the*
Bäsle *(little cousin). Pencil
drawing dating from 1777–8.*

soirées and private concerts. Now, at twenty-one, he had to behave as a petitioner, ingratiating himself with intermediaries and pleading his cause as best he could. An audience with the elector was engineered, but was not an elegant affair. Mozart had to wait in a small ante-room of the palace, and waylay the elector on his way to mass and a day's hunting. The elector was sympathetic, but 'did not have a vacancy'. Nevertheless, Mozart in his typical way responded to the music of the day. He was attracted by the new sonatas for piano and violin by the popular Dresden composer Joseph Schuster, and over the next few months wrote a set of six himself (K301–6).

Leopold bombarded his son with instructions, advising him to avoid 'heating drinks', reminding him to make sure to keep his boots in shape with boot-trees, interspersed with piteous statements such as 'My very life depends on yours, I am your old deserted father.' Actually, it would appear that Wolfgang did need looking after, since his letters from Munich describe wildly impractical plans. One moment, he outlined a Utopian scheme for a consortium of admirers to band together and pay him a regular pension. A few days later, he proposed living on in Munich with no official post at all, promising that he would always be invited out to dinner so would not need to pay for his food, and that he would drink water rather than wine in order to save money. Within another fortnight he was proposing that he should turn south instead of north, and travel to Naples to write operas. However, none of these plans came to fruition, so within a few days the pair moved on to Augsburg.

Augsburg was Leopold's home town. However, instead of being greeted with honour, Mozart was to suffer social humiliation and a severe blow to his pride. Leopold's brother Franz was a bookbinder, and did his duty by presenting the young composer to Jakob Langenmantel, the magistrate and city governor. Mozart was probably not aware that patricians in imperial free cities such as Augsburg considered themselves to be nobility, and quite distinct from the artisan classes to which his family belonged. He was embarrassed to find that when he played for Langenmantel, his uncle was expected to sit on a stool on the landing like a lackey. He had been instructed by his father to wear his papal cross while in Augsburg, since Leopold predicted it would win him honour and respect. The opposite was the case. Langenmantel's son and another arrogant youth made fun of Wolfgang and his papal order, asking him how much it was worth, what they had to do to get such a cross themselves, whether they could borrow it to be valued by the local jeweller, and so on. Mozart was mortified and unable to counter these bullies effectively. As far as we know, he never wore his cross again, or used the title of 'Chevalier' to which he was entitled.

Despite these setbacks, there were compensations in Augsburg. Mozart quickly formed a somewhat flirtatious relationship with his cousin Maria Anna Thekla (known as 'das Bäsle' or 'little cousin' in the family). The exact nature of their intimacy is not known, but later he was to write her a series of letters notorious for their coarse scatology. This is a typical example:

> Well, I wish you good night, but first shit in your bed and make it burst. Sleep soundly, my love, into your mouth your arse you'll shove ... Oh, my arse is burning like fire – what on earth does it mean? – perhaps some muck wants to come out? Why yes, muck, I know, see and smell you ... and ... what is that? Is it possible ... Ye Gods! Can I believe those ears of mine? Yes indeed, it is so – what a long melancholy note!

There is little sign that they went beyond playfulness, although scholars have argued on the basis of these letters and the *double entendres* they contain that there was a sexual relationship. Mozart's crude language is not unique to this correspondence; when he was in Italy, he signed off notes to his sister with phrases such as 'Keep well, and shit in your bed to make a mess of it.' Even his mother Maria Anna wrote playful vulgarities to her husband such as 'I wish you goodnight, my dear, but first shit in your bed and make it burst.' This would all appear to be

A view of the city of Munich painted in 1761 by Bernardo Bellotto.

part of a rumbustious, Rabelaisian streak which some contemporaries considered to be a Salzburg trait.

Mozart also made the acquaintance of a famous pianoforte maker, Johann Andreas Stein, whose instruments he much admired. With Stein's help he was able to play in two concerts, the second of which consisted entirely of his own music. The works included the Triple Concerto (K242) – played by Mozart, Stein and the cathedral organist – the Concerto in B flat (K238), his Munich Piano Sonata in D (K284), a symphony and other works. A eulogistic notice about the concert was published in a newspaper a few days later, asserting that 'everything was extraordinary, tasteful and admirable ... the rendering on the pianoforte so neat, so clean, so full of expression, and yet at the same time extraordinarily rapid, so that one hardly knew what to give attention to first, and all the hearers were enraptured'. Mozart was becoming recognized as a virtuoso of exceptional ability, combining taste with imaginative force. He also enjoyed himself a great deal when performing. His exuberance and pleasure at playing and improvising comes vividly to life in his description of a visit to a monastery in Augsburg:

> In the evening at supper I played my Strasbourg concerto [for violin, K216], which went like oil. Everyone praised my beautiful, pure tone ... Then the others whispered to the Dean that he should just hear me playing something in the organ style. I asked him to give me a theme. He declined, but one of the monks gave me one. I put it through its paces and in the middle (the fugue was in G minor) I started it off in the major key and played something quite lively, though in the same tempo; and after that the theme over again, but this time arse-ways. Finally it occurred to me, could I not use my lively tune as a theme for a fugue? I did not waste much time in asking, but did so at once, and it went as neatly as if Daser [a tailor] had fitted it.

He was able at last to please his father by earning some money, since the profit from the concert amounted to more than eighty gulden. Nevertheless, Leopold was critical about them spending as long as two weeks in Augsburg for only a couple of concerts, so the travellers soon moved further north up the Rhine to Mannheim.

Mannheim, Cannabich and the famous orchestra

Mozart must have approached Mannheim in a hopeful frame of mind. Mannheim was the principal residence of the Elector Palatine, Carl Theodor, an enthusiastic musician under whose patronage the Mannheim court orchestra had become famous throughout Europe. A Mannheim school of composers flourished, including members of the Stamitz family, Ignaz Holzbauer (the Kapellmeister at the time of Mozart's visit), and Christian Cannabich.

Cannabich was leader of the orchestra and director of instrumental music, and immediately established a warm relationship with the young composer. Within a few days, Mozart was spending much of his time with Cannabich and his family. He endeared himself by immediately beginning work on a piano sonata (K309 in C major) for the thirteen-year-old Rosa Cannabich, who was already an accomplished player. Cannabich helped to engineer performances for the elector and the court

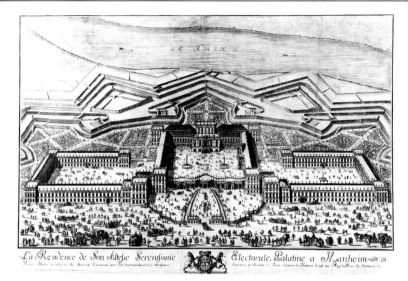

The palace of the Elector Palatine at Mannheim, built between 1720 and 1760.
Engraving after a drawing by the architect Jean Clemens de Froimont.

within a few days, and Mozart also played the organ in the court chapel. He became friendly with several musicians, including the oboe virtuoso Friedrich Ramm and the flautist Johann Wendling. For perhaps the first time in his life, Mozart mixed socially with musicians of talent, and he found their company engaging. He describes one evening at Cannabich's house (with Ramm and others) which they spent making up rhymes (on such subjects as muck, shitting and arse-licking). He presented Ramm with the oboe concerto (K271/314) he had recently completed in Salzburg, and the latter was delighted.

At the same time, he was not making money. In mid-November, he received his reward for performing at court. Instead of money it was a gold watch:

> Let me tell you, I now have five watches. I am therefore seriously thinking of having an additional watch pocket on each leg of my trousers so that

when I visit some great Lord, I shall wear both watches ... so that it will not occur to him to present me with another one.

Leopold was in a state of indecision about what his son should do now, and fired off instructions indiscriminately. One day he instructed his wife and son to move on directly to the court at Mainz, but in his next letter suggested they stay in Mannheim and try for employment there. As the weeks went by Leopold became increasingly distressed about the lack of income, and the debts that were building up. Chiefly, he objected to his son's lack of energy in actively seeking work. His model of how to behave on tour was simple:

> First find out from your landlord who is the Kapellmeister or music director of the place ... Arrange to be taken to him, or, if he is not too grand a person, ask him to call on you. You will then know at once whether giving a concert there is an expensive business, whether you can count on having a good harpsichord, whether an orchestra is available and whether there are many lovers of music ... you should do this on your arrival and without unpacking anything: Just put on a few fine rings and so forth, in case when you call you should find a harpsichord there and be asked to perform.

But Wolfgang was pleased to while away the time in good company. He kept Leopold's hopes alive with hints that the Elector Palatine was still deciding about whether or not to employ him, perhaps as piano teacher to his illegitimate children. He expressed a philosophical calm about his future that was to become an important part of his mature character. He was determined not to become anxious about matters over which he had little control, stating that 'I am simply prepared for anything and I am able ... to wait patiently for whatever may come.'

However, Leopold's more practical concerns would appear to have had some justification. His son had made little effort to take advantage of the unique musical situation in Mannheim. When he first arrived and was presented to the rather suspicious orchestra, he had boldly asserted, 'They probably think that because I am little and young, nothing great or mature can come out of me: but they will soon see.' But as far as we know, they did not 'see', because he had little involvement with the orchestra. Over the last three years he had composed numerous symphonies together with five violin concertos, but none of these was performed in Mannheim. Mozart was admired as a keyboard virtuoso, but probably only performed one of his concertos with the orchestra. Two factors may have been responsible. Firstly, he failed to make efforts to secure commissions. He did not take steps such as presenting his orchestral music to the elector, but appears to have waited passively for work to materialize. Secondly, he may have alienated some of the influential Mannheim musicians. He was particularly critical in his private letters of the composer and theorist Abbé Vogler ('a dreary musical jester, an exceedingly conceited and rather incompetent fellow'), and if such views were circulated in the city they might have caused him difficulties.

By mid-December 1777, the notion that he would be employed in Mannheim was finally abandoned, and it was agreed that he would travel on to Paris in the company of Johann Wendling and the oboist Friedrich Ramm. Maria Anna Mozart was to return to Salzburg via Augsburg, and much ink was expended on speculating about the best route. Meanwhile, Mozart was commissioned by an amateur musician, Ferdinand Dejean, to write three flute concertos and two flute quartets for 200 gulden. They moved to more suitable lodgings in the house of a privy councillor which were paid for by composition and piano lessons. Up to now, they had stayed in a miserable inn where Maria Anna was lonely and freezing cold, since they could not afford more than two fires each day. Matters appeared therefore to be improving. Then two events occurred that changed their plans dramatically.

The first was the death of Elector Maximilian, the ruler of Bavaria whom Mozart had met only three months before. This event thrust Mannheim and the Elector Palatine Carl Theodor into the forefront of European affairs. Maximilian had died without legitimate offspring, and his successor in the Wittelsbach dynasty was Carl Theodor. But Carl Theodor also had no legitimate children, so when he died both the Palatinate and Bavaria would fall to his heir, the duke of Zweibrücken. Empress Maria Theresa and her son and co-regent Emperor Joseph II were seriously concerned that this would create a large power bloc in south Germany, so they planned to annex Bavaria. Carl Theodor was no match militarily for the Austrians, so agreed to cede a substantial portion of Bavaria in exchange for unopposed accession. He left Mannheim on 1 January 1778 to take up residence in Munich. The other small German states were also powerless in the face of this Austrian aggression, and the Habsburgs assumed that Frederick the Great of Prussia was too old and ill to intervene. They reckoned, however, without Frederick's energy and determination, for by April 1778 a Prussian army of 100,000 men had been mobilized and advanced into Bohemia. The subsequent War of the Bavarian Succession continued for more than a year. Although it involved little actual fighting, the Austrians were forced to withdraw and had to give back most of the territory they had gained. The military mobilization threw the Mozarts' travel plans into jeopardy, while the transfer of the court to Munich robbed Mannheim of its major patrons. Under these circumstances, few people in authority had time to take an interest in the affairs of an itinerant young musician.

'I commend this poor, but excellent little Mlle Weber to your interest with all my heart'

The second momentous event was that Mozart came to know the Weber family. The father, Fridolin Weber, had been a civil servant, but by the time he met Mozart he was working in Mannheim as a music copyist. He and his wife had four daughters and a son. The third daughter was Mozart's future wife, Constanze, then just sixteen years old. However, at the time the young composer did not even notice Constanze, because he fell in love with her older sister, the eighteen-year-old Aloisia. Aloisia was first and foremost a promising opera singer, although she was also a competent pianist – she played one of the solo parts in a performance of the Triple Concerto later in the spring. Mozart went with Fridolin and Aloisia Weber to perform at an aristocratic residence outside Mannheim for two weeks, and when they returned, all thoughts of Paris were forgotten. He wrote to his father full of naive enthusiasm for Aloisia Weber, proposing to travel to Italy with her, to write operas for her in Venice and Verona, and make her famous as a prima donna. His excuse

for not going to Paris was that he had suddenly realized that Wendling
and Ramm were not good Christians and would be unsuitable company.

Leopold Mozart was absolutely appalled. He replied with a scathing
letter denouncing his son's lack of judgement, impracticality, betrayal of
his family and of his own talent:

> It depends solely on your good sense and your way of life whether you die
> as an ordinary musician, utterly forgotten by the world, or as a famous
> Kapellmeister, of whom posterity will read – whether, captured by some
> woman, you die bedded on straw in an attic full of starving children, or
> whether, after a Christian life spent in contentment, honour and renown,
> you leave this world with your family well provided for and your name
> respected by all.

Over the next few weeks, Leopold increased the pressure on his son. He
vividly described his own penurious state – having to survive in clothes
so shabby that he was embarrassed to be seen, wearing old and worn
shoes and no silk stockings. Nannerl Mozart was obliged to give up the
fifty gulden she had carefully saved over the years to subsidize her
brother, while Leopold became more and more depressed.

Faced with this onslaught, Mozart had little choice but to concede. In
fact, his later letters from Mannheim appear much less affected by the
forthcoming separation from Aloisia than one would have imagined if she
really had been the great love of his life (as has been asserted by many
biographers in the past). But his travel plans had to be changed. Wendling
and Ramm had already left Mannheim, so Mozart's mother was now to
travel with him. Meanwhile, Wolfgang had only partly managed to complete the commission for flute compositions for Dejean. He finished one
concerto (K313 in G major), and transcribed his new oboe concerto for
flute (K314). He also wrote two quartets, only one of which (K285 in D
major) is known to survive in its entirety. His excuse was that 'It is not
surprising that I have not been able to finish them, for I never have a single
quiet hour here ... Moreover, you know that I become quite powerless
whenever I am obliged to write for an instrument which I cannot bear.' It
is true that he was simultaneously composing arias for Aloisia Weber, Anton
Raaff, the celebrated though ageing tenor, and Elisabeth Wendling, but

Aloisia Lange (née Weber) painted in 1784 by Johann Baptist von Lampi.

there is little doubt that he would have polished off the flute commission if he had not been emotionally so distracted. The quartet K285 shows no signs of Mozart's supposed dislike for the flute, for it is a delicate and well-balanced piece, containing an adagio of exquisite melancholy. These compositions delayed the departure from Mannheim by several more weeks, but on 12 March there was a farewell concert at Cannabich's house. Two days later they finally set out for Paris.

Disappointment in Paris

They arrived in Paris on 23 March 1778, and Mozart quickly set about making himself known. He made the acquaintance of Joseph Legros, a tenor who created leading roles in several of Gluck's French operas. Legros was director of the famous Concert Spiиtuel concert series, and immediately put Mozart to work adapting a choral piece by the Mannheim Kapellmeister, Holzbauer. A *sinfonia concertante* for flute, oboe, horn, bassoon and orchestra was planned for Mozart's friends Wendling and Ramm, and there was even talk of an opera.

However, Mozart soon found that Paris was a large and difficult city in which to make his way. The aristocracy were indifferent to his talent, as was illustrated by his treatment at the hands of the duchesse de Chabot. He called at the Paris residence of the duchess, and was kept waiting in an unheated room for half an hour. When the duchess arrived she asked him to play, but then sat down with her companions to draw and took no further notice as he struggled to perform effectively with numb fingers. This was a far cry from the enthusiasm which had greeted him as a child. Mozart also failed to obtain an audience at court. France had been ruled for the past four years by Louis XVI and Queen Marie Antoinette, the Habsburg princess who was only a year older than Mozart. There had been a period of disharmony resulting in part from the king's impotence, during which the royal couple had led almost separate lives. However, a visit from Emperor Joseph II in 1777 had led to reconciliation, and at the time of Mozart's visit, Marie Antoinette was pregnant for the first time. She was leading a quiet life at Versailles. The summer of 1778 was unusually hot in Paris, and because her pregnancy kept her awake, Marie Antoinette took long nocturnal walks round the gardens accompanied by the musicians of the Chapelle. The arrival of a young Austrian virtuoso might have seemed auspicious. Yet despite his nationality and reputation, Mozart was not invited to perform at court.

One reason was that Parisians were in the grip of a musical controversy between the supporters of Gluck's operas and the new Italian style, typified by Niccolò Piccinni. Mozart therefore had competitors of a far higher reputation than himself, and he may once again have alienated local musicians with his uncompromising views. He was critical of French singers ('they hardly deserve the name, for they don't sing'), of the French language ('detestable for music'), and French taste. Intrigues began, and his sinfonia concertante was not performed. Half of the music he wrote for Holzbauer's work was cut, and the opera plan came to nothing.

Nevertheless, he did compose the Symphony in D major (K297) which received its première at the Concert Spirituel on 18 June. Mozart thought carefully about how to create a work suitable for his French audience. He used a large orchestra that included clarinets for the first time, as well as the usual woodwind and brass. He paid particular attention to the symphonies of the Mannheim composer Carl Toeschi, who had recently scored marked success in Paris, and took good care to begin the symphony with the type of unison passage that the Parisians liked. Nevertheless, he was unusually nervous about the reception of the 'Paris' Symphony. In fact it seems to have gone down well, although the impresario Legros thought that the Andante was too long and complicated, and insisted that it be replaced for a repeat performance in August.

A few other works were completed while Mozart was in Paris, including a set of six violin sonatas that had been begun in Mannheim, the delightful Concerto for Flute and Harp, and the ballet music *Les petits riens*. Two important minor-key works were also written: the passionate Piano Sonata in A minor (K310) [CD 1] and the remarkable Violin Sonata in E minor. However, Mozart's lack of success, coupled with longing for Aloisia Weber, led to despondency, and on 29 May he told his father, 'I often wonder whether life is worth living – I am neither hot nor cold – and don't find much pleasure in anything.'

Worse was to come. In the second half of June, Mozart's mother Maria Anna fell ill. She probably contracted typhus fever, then a condition that was all too prevalent in poor, crowded and unhygienic cities. After a two-week illness, she died on 3 July, aged fifty-seven. Maria Anna Mozart has remained a shadowy figure. We know little of her views of life, beliefs, ambitions, or even her musical tastes. Nevertheless, she was supportive of her son, putting up with loneliness, isolation, cold and ill-health in unfamiliar countries without complaint. Her relationship with Leopold, insofar as we can assess it on the evidence of their letters, was companionable and full of humour, and he did not patronize her despite his greater education and sophistication.

Her death was the first real tragedy that Mozart had encountered in his life, and he was left isolated. He responded with an unexpected maturity and thoughtfulness. The illness leading up to Maria Anna's death had arisen between letters to Salzburg, so Leopold and Nannerl had no inkling that anything was wrong. The announcement of her death would therefore have come as a devastating blow. Consequently, Mozart sat down a few hours after her death and wrote two letters. The first was to Leopold and Nannerl, and stated that Maria Anna was seriously ill, that there was hope for her recovery, but that they might have to prepare for the worst. He then continued the letter with a description of his usual activities, an extraordinary act of self-control that helped to defuse the seriousness of his warnings. A second letter was to the family's intimate friend the Abbé Bullinger, telling him the truth and asking him to break the news as he thought appropriate. It was only a few days later that Mozart told the complete story to his father and sister, movingly offering them the consolation of belief in God and being reunited in the afterlife. Yet despite this sensitivity, there is a curious detachment about the letters that Mozart wrote in the weeks following his mother's death. It was only after Leopold's demands for further details that his son gave him a proper account of the circumstances. Moreover, he did not even mention his recent bereavement in letters to Aloisia and her father, even though one might have expected it to be uppermost in his mind.

Mozart moved in to lodge with his old champion Baron Grimm and his companion Madame d'Épinay soon after Maria Anna's death, and found himself in a quandary. On the one hand, Leopold was now demanding that he return to Salzburg. He claimed, 'If you stay away, I shall die much sooner, and ... if I could have the joy of having you with me, I should live several years longer.' Mozart himself expressed a frank dislike of Paris, and had a strong desire to leave. On the other hand, the notion of returning to Salzburg was abhorrent. His greatest wish was to return to Mannheim to see Aloisia Weber once again, but he was reluctant to say so openly.

Meanwhile, the situation in Paris deteriorated. He was so short of money that he pawned his dead mother's watch. He became estranged from Baron Grimm. Grimm was an adherent of the Piccinni camp, but Mozart was not prepared to share this enthusiasm. Grimm was also critical of the young man's passivity, telling Leopold: 'He is too trusting, too inactive, too easy to catch, too little intent on the means that may lead to fortune. To make an impression here one has to be artful, enterprising, daring. To make his fortune I wish he had but half his talent and twice as much shrewdness, and then I should not worry about him.'

Mozart prepared to embark on the return journey to Germany with his usual lack of haste, while Leopold sent ever more peremptory commands. Baron Grimm was keen to bustle him off, so his departure at the end of September was undignified. Both Leopold and Grimm were convinced that Wolfgang would return directly to Salzburg by way of Strasbourg and Munich. However, the young composer was once more to surprise them with his independence.

The slow return to Salzburg

The first stops on the eastward journey were Nancy and Strasbourg, where Mozart played a solo concert and two poorly attended orchestral concerts. Here, he also learned that Aloisia Weber had been awarded a contract to join the opera company in Munich. He might have been expected to continue south directly to Munich, but instead he turned north so as to revisit Mannheim. The reasons are not clear, other than his liking for the city. Aloisia had moved, the court and all its musicians had transferred to Munich, and even his friend Cannabich had gone. However, Frau Cannabich was still there, and it was with her that Mozart stayed. He quickly established a warm and loving relationship with her, calling her 'one of my best and truest friends'. It is possible that after the death of his mother, he found comfort in the company of this undemanding middle-aged woman, and sympathy for his difficult situation. He also had a new musical enthusiasm, which was to write a *melodrama*. This was a piece in which dramatic text was spoken over expressive music, and was a speciality of the Bohemian composer Georg Benda. He was excited by the dramatic effect of such works, and the way the meaning of the text was accentuated. Although his plans came to nothing in 1778, he was to write two sections in this style in the unfinished Singspiel *Zaide*, the first of which is particularly moving.

Leopold was beside himself when he learned that his son had gone to Mannheim. Not only was he disobeying explicit instructions, he was also putting at risk the post of court organist in Salzburg that Leopold had secured for him. Leopold had tried every tactic to persuade his son to come home, appealing to his sense of duty, his love for his family, and his sense of pity. Now he threatened to humiliate Wolfgang by writing to Frau Cannabich informing her of all their debts (amounting to nearly 900 gulden) and Wolfgang's ingratitude. Even so, it was not until 9 December that Mozart was prised away, and he then spent two weeks at a monastery before reaching Munich.

Here further unhappiness awaited him, since he found that his feelings for Aloisia were not reciprocated. It is possible that her affection had never been strong, but that his own enthusiasm coupled with the jesting complicity of acquaintances had magnified the relationship in his mind to something greater than it was. Many commentators have regarded his rejection by Aloisia to be a critical event, and his subsequent marriage to Constanze a poor substitute. But there is little evidence of this. In later years he worked extensively with Aloisia without any apparent difficulty, and he was also on good terms with her future husband, the actor Joseph Lange. Nonetheless, coming as it did at the end of this unsuccessful and sad

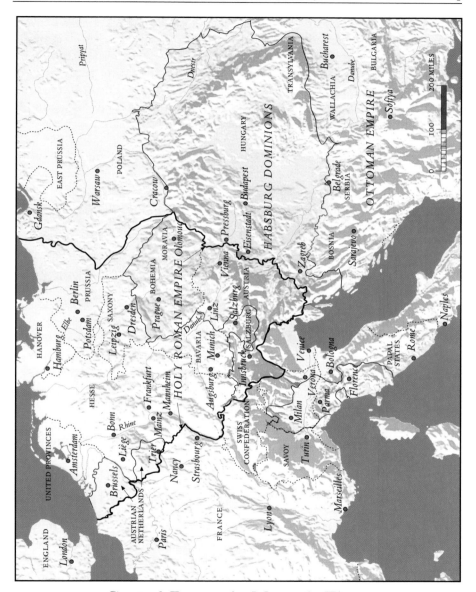

Central Europe in Mozart's Time

The black line shows the boundaries of the Holy Roman Empire,
while the Habsburg domains are shown in grey

year, her coolness was a blow. Mozart stayed on in Munich for three weeks, and completed the final stage of the journey back to his home town on 15 January 1779, two weeks before his twenty-third birthday.

The year 1778 had probably been one of the least productive of Mozart's life. Between his mother's death in early July and the return to Salzburg, he completed virtually no works that we know of. He certainly learned both from the music he had heard, and from the style and professionalism of the Mannheim orchestra, but these lessons were only to bear fruit in later years. At a personal level, the journey marked a profound change in the most important relationship of his early life. Hitherto, Mozart and his father had been united in their plans and goals, and he had received unqualified support from Leopold in all his actions. This situation changed dramatically. During these months away from Salzburg, Wolfgang and Leopold had frequent disagreements. Leopold had reacted angrily; he had accused his son of lying, of being lazy and selfish, and had threatened publicly to humiliate him. Yet it is interesting that even in the worst phases of their relationship, Leopold never once suggested that his son's success owed anything to his own efforts. Other fathers, faced with what they regarded as a betrayal by their creations, might have been more spiteful. But Leopold never took credit for his son's genius, which he continued to regard as God-given talent. In this way, he sustained Wolfgang's core of musical confidence and self-esteem. Mozart in turn continued to show great reliance on Leopold, calling him 'most beloved father and my truest friend', even if he had begun to recognize that his way through life would increasingly draw him away from his father.

CHAPTER 7

Salzburg, Munich and *Idomeneo*

Mozart moved back into the family apartment in the Dancing Master's House on the Hannibal-Platz in January 1779. He was appointed cathedral organist with a salary of 450 gulden, and was obliged to give keyboard lessons to the choirboys as well. The debts that he had

Portrait of the Mozart family by Johann Nepomuk della Croce, 1780–81. Mozart sits at the keyboard in a wig next to his elaborately coiffed sister, while Leopold holds his violin. Mozart's mother is represented posthumously in the central roundel.

accrued over the Mannheim and Paris tour totalled several hundred gulden, and were a major embarrassment for a supposedly successful young musician. For many people, this ignominious return to the despised archbishop's service, following a series of personal and professional disappointments, would have led to despondency and inactivity. Paradoxically however, the next eighteen months in Salzburg were a period of great musical creativity. It is as if it was only now, harnessed to the routine of the cathedral and court, that he had time to assimilate the experiences of the past months.

There were many times in his life when contact with new music or performance styles inspired him to compose in that same form, as in the case of the violin sonatas he wrote in 1777 and 1778 after hearing Schuster's work, or the set of string quartets composed in 1773 after hearing Haydn's opus 20 in Vienna. Now in 1779, Mozart was stimulated by the orchestral and choral music he had heard in Mannheim and Paris, and the result was a series of major works for large forces. For the church, there were the two extended settings of the vespers (K321 and K339), the second of which was the *Vesperae solennes de confessore*, with its glorious soprano aria 'Laudate dominum'. There were also two masses, the first being the 'Coronation' Mass (K317), one of the finest of his religious works. It received this name because it was conducted by Salieri at the coronation of Emperor Leopold II in Prague in 1791, a mark of the great esteem in which it was held even then. For the orchestra, there were two symphonies in 1779, K318 and K319, that soon became popular. K318 in G major was later used in Vienna as an overture for an opera by another composer, and was heard in Frankfurt, Augsburg and Prague within a few years. K319 in B flat major was published in Vienna within a few years, and may have been one of the earliest mature works played in London. These were followed by the 'Posthorn' Serenade in the summer, and the scintillating three-movement C major Symphony (K338) one year later. The concerto was not neglected either. Shortly after his return to Salzburg, Mozart wrote the delightful Concerto for two Pianos (K365). This was presumably composed for him to perform with his sister, and is a work of poise, wit and delicacy. Then in the autumn came the sublime Sinfonia concertante for Violin and Viola (K364), one of the most profound of all his compositions [CD 2].

Mozart's work with the orchestra was made easier by the fact that the post of Kapellmeister was vacant during this period, so Leopold was the senior musician in Salzburg. During 1779 and 1780, the Mozarts were very much in charge of the orchestra and its activities. The family also took to ambitious music-making in their own apartment. The best documented example of a domestic concert of this kind took place on Easter Saturday 1780. Symphonies by Mozart started and finished the programme. In between there were two arias by him, together with vocal works by Antonio Salieri, the Italian Pasquale Anfossi and the French composer Grétry. It is apparent that the family kept fully up to date with European developments on the musical stage, despite the limited opportunities in Salzburg.

We know very little of Mozart's emotional life over this period, but he seems to have rejoined the old social circle smoothly enough. They went to mass almost every day, played skittles and card games, and one of the regular rituals was a Sunday shooting competition, for which the participants prepared ribald or humorous targets. The routine was greatly enlivened by the arrival of Johann Böhm's theatrical troupe in Salzburg. Böhm was no provincial impresario, but a distinguished manager and competent musician who had appeared extensively in Vienna. The company was based at the Ballhaus Theatre situated across the Hannibal-Platz from the Mozarts' apartment, and the family were given free passes to attend whenever they wished. The repertoire was wide-ranging, and included operas as well as spoken comedies and tragedies. During the season in Salzburg, they almost certainly put on plays by Shakespeare, Voltaire, Goldoni and Gozzi, together with operas by Gluck, Piccinni, Grétry and Paisiello.

Mozart delighted in the theatre. In an earlier letter, he had told his father: 'I have an inexpressible longing to write another opera ... I have only to hear an opera discussed, I have only to sit in a theatre, hear the orchestra tuning their instruments – Oh, I am quite beside myself at once.' He and his sister went several times a week, and even sat in on rehearsals. He soon became involved with the company. One project was to adapt the Munich opera *La finta giardiniera* so that it could be presented as a Singspiel in German. Mozart revised and extended the music he had composed for the play *Thamos, König in Ägypten* (*Thamos, King of Egypt*), and this was later used by Böhm in other productions. The other work that dates from this period is the unfinished Singspiel now known as *Zaide*. This was composed to a libretto by the Salzburg musician and writer Johann Andreas Schachtner, an old friend of the family. Its genesis

Dorothea Wendling, the wife of Mozart's friend the flautist Johann Wendling, and the first Ilia in Idomeneo.

is not known. It may have been planned for performance by the Böhm company, but some scholars now believe that Mozart intended it for the newly-formed German opera company in Vienna. In any event it was never completed, although fifteen musical numbers survive. This is a great pity, since *Zaide* contains wonderful music, notably the melodramas modelled after Benda, the exquisite aria for Zaide, 'Ruhe sanft', and the fine trio at the end of Act I.

In the summer of 1780, a much more exciting prospect arose with the commission to compose the carnival season opera seria for Munich. It is probable that this commission was a late fruit of the favourable impression he had made on Elector Carl Theodor in Mannheim nearly three years earlier. Not only was this a prestigious commission, it was also an opportunity to leave Salzburg and perhaps even find permanent employment in Munich. The subject of the opera was Idomeneo, the tragic king of Crete. The story had been set before by an Italian composer, but the libretto that Mozart used was prepared by the Salzburg court chaplain Gianbattista Varesco.

Work on the opera began in the summer of 1780. Fortunately, Mozart could prepare many of the arias in Salzburg, since he knew a number of the soloists already. The flautist Wendling's wife Dorothea played the part of Ilia, while his sister-in-law Elisabeth was Elettra. The title role was taken by Anton Raaff, the famous tenor who had been a staunch friend in Mannheim and Paris. The composition was well under way when a second theatrical troupe took up residence in Salzburg in September 1780. This one was directed by an actor who was to play an important part in Mozart's later years in Vienna, Emanuel Schikaneder (the author of *The Magic Flute* and the first Papageno). The versatile Schikaneder had toured widely in southern Germany for a number of

years, writing plays and light operas, acting, singing and dancing. He soon joined
the Mozart social circle, participating in
their shooting parties and endearing himself to Leopold. However, Wolfgang himself was preoccupied with his opera, and
in early November was granted six weeks'
leave to attend to its production.

Munich: 'The most happy time of his life'

Idomeneo was produced under the most
favourable circumstances, and the composer's widow later said that these weeks
in Munich had been among the happiest
of his life. Aloisia Weber was no longer in
the opera company, since she had been
given a contract in Vienna, but this evidently did not trouble him at all. The

The tenor Anton Raaff, drawn and engraved by G. F. Touchemolin.

orchestra in Munich was of course the celebrated Mannheim band, and
Mozart was delighted to renew acquaintance with Christian Cannabich.
He also worked with one of the most innovative production teams of the
era, the designer Lorenzo Quaglio and the ballet master Claude Le Grand.

Discussions with this group soon led Mozart to demand changes
to the libretto. These were relayed to Varesco by Leopold, and the
correspondence provides a unique insight into the composer's working
methods. Mozart was a consummate man of the theatre. He had a sure
sense of drama, and exact notions of how particular speeches would
translate into effective music. At the forefront of his thinking was always
the issue of dramatic credibility, and maintaining the pace of the action.
For example, Varesco had included a spoken aside in an aria designed
for Ilia. Mozart considered this quite acceptable in a recitative, but not
in an aria, where the words would have to be repeated. Later, he
criticized the length of the speech given to the subterranean voice

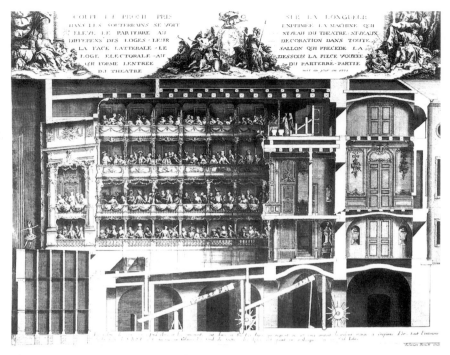

The Residenztheater, also known as the Cuvilliés theatre, in Munich. It was here that Idomeneo *was first performed in 1781. Engraving by Valerian Funck after François Cuvilliés and Ignaz Günther.*

emanating from the altar of Neptune's temple in Act III. Thinking, no doubt, of recent productions of *Hamlet* that he had attended either in Salzburg or Munich, he argued:

> Picture to yourself the theatre, and remember that the voice must be terrifying – must penetrate – that the audience must believe that it really exists. Well, how can this effect be produced if the speech is too long, for in this case the listeners will become more and more convinced that it means nothing. If the speech of the ghost in *Hamlet* were not so long, it would be far more effective.

Idomeneo is also remarkable for the storm music which surely accompanied some spectacular stage effects, and for the electrifying choruses. It is our loss that Viennese opera buffa made little use of stage choruses, since Mozart had few opportunities in later years to display his fine dramatic deployment of them.

Not everything in the production went his way. Unfortunately, he had to contend with a castrato in the role of Idamante who had neither theatrical flair nor musical skill. Mozart told his father that the poor man, Vincenzo dal Prato, 'is utterly useless ... His voice would not be so bad if he did not produce it in his throat and larynx.

'Maria Theresa's Last Day'. A commemorative engraving by H. Löschenkohl, issued in February 1781.

But he has no intonation, no method, no feeling.' Nor were matters helped by Anton Raaff being such a wooden actor. At the time he took the title role, Raaff was more than sixty-five years old. His age at least was appropriate for the tragic, isolated figure of Idomeneo. Mozart made great efforts to suit his music to Raaff's declining abilities. When he had written an aria for the tenor in 1778, he was quite candid about the need to tailor his music to his singer's strengths.

> One must treat a man like Raaff in a particular way. I chose those words on purpose, because I knew that he already had an aria on them: so of course he will sing mine with greater facility and more pleasure. I asked him to tell me candidly if he did not like it or if it did not suit his voice, adding that I would alter it if he wished or even compose another. 'God forbid,' he said, 'the aria must remain just as it is, for nothing could be finer. But please shorten it a little, for I am no longer able to sustain my notes.' 'Most gladly,' I replied, 'as much as you like. I made it a little long on purpose, for it is always easy to cut down, but not so easy to lengthen'.

There was a setback at the end of November when the Empress Maria Theresa died. Such a major event demanded a period of official mourning, so there was concern that the production would be postponed.

The stage design of the Temple of Neptune in Idomeneo *made by Lorenzo Quaglio.*

However, rehearsals were already under way, and the mourning period was set for six weeks, making feasible the première at the end of January. The musicians of the orchestra were delighted with the work, and such was the interest that the elector himself attended a rehearsal in late December. 'Who would believe that such great things could be hidden in so small a head?' was his comment. Yet back in Salzburg, Leopold was concerned about the success of the work. Unlike earlier years in which he had been so confident of a positive reception, Leopold clearly felt that the music was *avant garde*, moving in uncharted and unpopular directions. He also had very sensible ideas about keeping the musicians well motivated while learning the piece:

> But do your best to keep the whole orchestra in good humour; flatter them, and, by praising them, keep them all well-disposed towards you. For I know your style of composition – it requires unusually close attention from the players of every type of instrument; and to keep the whole orchestra at such a pitch of industry and alertness for at least three hours is no joke. Each performer, even the most inferior viola player, is deeply touched by personal praise and becomes much more zealous and attentive, while a little courtesy of this kind only costs you a word or two.

The première approached, but still Mozart demanded modifications to the libretto. A particularly troublesome section involved the later

Pastel portrait of Elisabeth ('Lisl') Wendling, another member of the talented musical family. She was the first Elettra in Idomeneo.

scenes of Act III, and the final aria for Idomeneo. Demands for changes in verses, phrases and even in single words went back and forth between Munich and Salzburg, and it is no wonder that Varesco became irritated. However, perhaps the most astonishing aspect of the production of *Idomeneo* was Mozart's ruthless editing in pursuit of dramatic coherence. Not only were recitatives shortened, he was prepared to sacrifice the music he himself had so carefully crafted, if he felt it was necessary. Elettra's splendidly furious aria 'D'Oreste, d'Aiace' was cut, together with much of the music for the secondary character of Arbace. Even the Act III aria for Idomeneo, 'Torna la pace al core', which had been rewritten twice by Varesco, was jettisoned as superfluous to the action. Seldom can music of such great quality and beauty have been set aside by a composer on his own recommendation in the interests of the production as a whole.

Leopold, Nannerl and several Salzburg acquaintances came to Munich for the première in late January 1781. We do not know very much about the reception of *Idomeneo*. At least five performances were scheduled, but it was repeated only twice. The production certainly failed in one important respect, in that Mozart was not offered employment by the elector. Perhaps Leopold was right, and the music was too complex and subtle for the Munich establishment. Nevertheless, the composer remained very attached to the piece, and supervised a revival in a concert performance in Vienna in 1786. The score remains one of the most vivid and dramatic in all opera seria. Mozart took full advantage of the virtuoso Mannheim orchestra to create billiant wind *concertante* sections, and the rich sonority of the work is unique in his output.

Archbishop Colloredo did not travel to Munich to attend the work of his employee. Instead he left Salzburg in the spring for an extended visit to Vienna. Mozart had outstayed his leave in Munich, and the archbishop demanded that he join the senior musicians of the establishment, and be available to entertain his guests in the capital. Accordingly, Mozart did not return to Salzburg after *Idomeneo*, but travelled directly to Vienna. Unbeknown to him, he was never to live in the town of his birth again.

CHAPTER 8

The Vienna of Joseph II

Vienna in early 1781 was on the threshold of an extraordinary decade. The death of Empress Maria Theresa at last gave her son and co-regent Joseph II the opportunity to act according to his own beliefs. Over the next nine years, he undertook a series of radical reforms that astonished Europe and earned him the admiration of intellectuals and progressive thinkers. History, however, has regarded him as more of an enlightened despot than a genuine revolutionary, for he promulgated enlightened beliefs while at the same time riding roughshod over opposing views.

The legislation initiated by Joseph affected many aspects of life. One of his first acts was to reform the church, suppressing rich landowning monasteries, reducing clerical privilege and limiting the baroque operatic splendour of church services. He allowed the practice of non-Catholic faiths, and gave the large Jewish population in the empire freedom of movement and access to jobs and education. The legal system was

The Michaelerplatz in Vienna, engraved by Carl Schütz in 1783. On the extreme right is the Burgtheater where Mozart gave several concerts, and where the first performances were given of The Seraglio, The Marriage of Figaro, *and* Così fan tutte.

simplified, the nobility lost their privileged status and torture was prohibited. Education was expanded with the aim of compulsory schooling for all children between six and twelve years old; poor relief was introduced, and a comprehensive public health programme was set in train. Some of his most important reforms were in the economic sphere, where proposals to better the lot of peasants were coupled with a rapid increase in manufacturing capacity that went some way towards bringing the monarchy into the industrial age. In order to promote these changes, Joseph found it necessary to create an effective central administration. A new class of minor nobility, councillors, civil servants and rich merchants emerged in Vienna, and was to become an important source of intellectual stimulation and patronage for artists such as Mozart.

Joseph's legislative zeal may have set the broad agenda, but of greater

Emperor Joseph II seated at the keyboard, with his two unmarried sisters Marie Anna and Elisabeth. Oil painting by Joseph Hauzinger, before 1780.

relevance to Mozart and his circle were the changes in Vienna itself. There was a dramatic relaxation of censorship, as the emperor believed that freedom of speech and publication would favour his reform programme. Numerous coffee-houses were established, to which people went to talk, read journals and play billiards. The *salons* of the Viennese intelligentsia became renowned throughout Europe for the openness with which political issues were discussed and radical views were expressed. High-born aristocrats, soldiers, administrators and cultivated bourgeois met in an egalitarian atmosphere to discuss the issues of the day and to listen to music.

These changes were reinforced by the behaviour of the emperor himself. Unlike other monarchs of the late eighteenth century, Joseph was a man of simple tastes who disliked ceremony and grandeur. He took personal interest in the running of the city, arranging improvements to the roads and lighting with as much attention as he paid to major issues of state. He opened the imperial parks at the Prater and Augarten to the public, making them the places of general entertainment and recreation that they remain to this day. He liked to mingle in society rather than be separated by precedent and protocol. He dressed informally, and lived modestly in a villa in the Augarten, rarely using the magnificent palace of Schönbrunn. Dr John Moore, a Scottish physician and writer who travelled through Europe as companion to the young duke of Hamilton, was astonished by the emperor:

> His manner is affable, obliging and perfectly free from the reserved and lofty deportment assumed by some on account of high birth. This monarch converses with all the ease and affability of a private gentleman, and gradually seduces others to talk with the same ease to him.

In many ways, the Vienna of the Josephinian decade seemed to provide a healthy compromise between the social forces of the day. In comparison with the mercantile self-confidence of England it was cultivated and sophisticated; set against the frenetic hedonism of Venice it was mild and sober; while in contrast to the violent schisms between aristocrat and revolutionary in France it was tolerant. On leaving Vienna after an extended stay, Dr Moore concluded:

> I have never passed my time more agreeably than since I came to Vienna. There is not such a constant round of amusements as to fill up a man's time without any plan or occupation of his own; and yet there is enough to satisfy any mind not perfectly vacant and dependent on external objects.

Mozart was fortunate to arrive in Vienna at the birth of this new era, and he benefited from the combination of aristocratic and middle-class

A pavilion in the Prater, the large park in Vienna opened to the public by Joseph II. The emperor is depicted riding in the carriage on the left with Count Rosenberg, director of the court theatres in Vienna. Detail of an engraving by Johann Ziegler, 1783.

patronage that emerged. The notion that people should be judged on their personal merits and talents and not on their birth and background did much to soothe the social humiliations of the past years in Salzburg. He was also lucky that the Viennese were so passionately fond of music. The evening parties of the nobility and middle classes provided opportunities to perform, and amateur musicians flourished. Publishers hastened to supply the market with chamber works and with keyboard reductions of popular operatic pieces. Musicians also found employment in the well-attended theatres of the city. The two principal theatres were the Burgtheater and the Kärntnerthor theatre. The Burgtheater was part of the building complex of the royal palace, so was somewhat smaller but more prestigious. It was the traditional home of the Italian opera, but in 1778 Joseph had disbanded the Italian troupe and replaced it with the National Singspiel in the hope of encouraging German art. The

The Kärntnerthor theatre, the second of the two court-controlled theatres in Vienna. Mozart played in several concerts there, and The Seraglio *was frequently heard. This engraving was made in 1827.*

experiment continued until 1783, when the Italian opera was reinstated. When Mozart arrived in Vienna in 1781, both opera and spoken drama were presented at the Burgtheater every day except Fridays, while the Kärntnerthor was leased to various troupes and impresarios. In addition, there were a number of theatres in the suburbs of Vienna that put on more popular entertainments such as light operas, farces and pantomimes. Three or four of the highest aristocracy, notably Prince Auersperg and Count Johann Baptist Esterházy, maintained their own private theatres, where performances were given by the nobility supported by professional actors.

The senior Kapellmeister in Vienna in 1781 was Giuseppe Bonno. He was now seventy years old, having served the court since 1739, and was no longer very active. Gluck was a similar age but not yet ready for retirement, since he had recently completed *Iphigénie en Tauride* and *Echo et Narcisse*. The most prominent composer of the younger generation was Antonio Salieri. Italian by birth, Salieri had spent most of his life in Vienna, had been appointed court composer in 1774, and was conductor of the Italian opera both in the 1770s and again in the 1780s. He was a favourite of Joseph II, and thus came to have a great influence on Viennese musical life during the Josephinian decade. His assistant at the opera was Ignaz Umlauf, a composer for whom Mozart had little time. These individuals were based in Vienna and worked for the court. Other musicians such as Joseph Haydn and Carl Dittersdorf were in the employ of aristocratic households, so were only present in the capital during the season.

Like other eighteenth-century cities, Vienna had definite seasons during which the aristocracy was in residence. Many of the nobility spent the summer and autumn on their country estates. They returned in late autumn, and the carnival season lasted from the day after Christmas until Shrove Tuesday. The theatres were closed for opera and plays during Lent, but continued to be used for concerts. The theatre orchestras also became available, so Lent was a vital period for performers such as Mozart. The normal season continued after Easter for a few more months, and some high-ranking individuals remained in the city for most of the year.

An unfinished portrait of Mozart by Joseph Lange, the actor husband of Aloisia Weber. The portrait dates from 1789/90, and was considered by contemporaries to be among the best likenesses of the composer.

One can well imagine that compared with the lively winter and spring in the capital, the summer months spent on the remote estates of the aristocracy would have dragged. It is no wonder that Joseph Haydn, obliged to spend several months every year in the isolated vastness of Eszterháza in his capacity as Kapellmeister to Prince Nicholas Esterházy, wrote so longingly for the society of Vienna:

> Here I sit in my wilderness; forsaken, like some poor orphan, almost without human society; melancholy, dwelling on the memory of past glorious days ... and who can tell when those happy hours may return? Those charming meetings? Where the whole circle have but one heart and one soul – all those delightful musical evenings, which can only be remembered and not described.

CHAPTER 9

Emotional Emancipation and Marriage

It is no exaggeration to say that the last decade of Mozart's life transformed the landscape of music, and represents one of the most remarkable periods of sustained effort, imagination and creativity known in any artist. Over these years, Mozart composed six operas, at least four of which are recognized as among the greatest ever written, the Requiem and the great C minor Mass. He also wrote seventeen piano concertos that virtually created the genre and remain among its supreme achievements, six symphonies, ten string quartets and five quintets, piano sonatas, trios and quartets, and a large number of other works for voice, chamber group and orchestra. In total, he completed more than 130 major compositions during this period. This is all the more astonishing when one realizes that Mozart was not a recluse working in splendid isolation, but had a busy and eventful life. He earned his living as a piano virtuoso, teaching and performing, mounting concerts and organizing tours. He was gregarious and actively involved in the cultural and intellectual world of Vienna, and his emotional and domestic life was far from tranquil. He fell in love and was married, lived in cramped apartments with small children, experienced periods of intense conflict with his father, bouts of serious illness for himself and his wife, and suffered the death of four children, and times of acute financial difficulty. Yet transcending all this was an extraordinary drive and energy to write music.

Mozart arrived in Vienna on 16 March 1781, not long after his twenty-fifth birthday. Later that same day he was already involved in a concert as part of the archbishop's suite. He was lodged along with other members of the Salzburg household, and immediately felt the humiliation of his position.

> We lunch about twelve o'clock, unfortunately somewhat too early for me. Our party consists of the two valets, that is, the body and soul attendants of His Worship, the contrôleur, Herr Zetti [the Archbishop's private messenger], the confectioner, two cooks, Ceccarelli [the castrato], Brunetti [the violinist], and – my insignificant self. By the way, the two valets sit at the top of the table, but at least I have the honour of being placed above the cooks. Well, I almost believe myself back in Salzburg! A good deal of silly, coarse joking goes on at table ...

Countess Wilhelmine Thun. A silhouette by Johann Friedrich Anthing, dating from 1788.

Mozart's remark about the time of day was not trivial, because the dinner hour reflected subtle social distinctions. Twelve o'clock was the lunchtime of the common people, while the middle classes ate at one o'clock and the nobility at two or even later.

He was determined to separate himself from the less sophisticated professional musicians of the Salzburg establishment. He soon found that his playing was admired by the aristocracy, and he was taken up by the influential Countess Wilhelmine Thun, whose *salon* was famed throughout Europe. In less than a week he was able to tell his father: 'I have lunched twice with Countess Thun and go there almost every day. She is the most charming and most lovable lady I have ever met;

Portrait of Constanze Mozart by her brother-in-law Joseph Lange, dating from 1789/90. Her marriage to Mozart in August 1782 sealed his escape from Leopold's influence.

and I am very high in her favour.' He played at a number of gatherings, culminating in his appearance at the concert of the Society of Musicians at the Kärntnerthor theatre. The society was a musicians' benevolent organization for the support of widows and orphans, and performers gave their services without charge. Mozart played a concerto, borrowing the Countess Thun's fortepiano for the occasion, and according to his letter home, 'I had to begin all over again, because there was no end to the applause. Well, how much do you suppose I should make if I were to give a concert of my own, now that the public has got to know me?' He was particularly frustrated that an obligation to perform for the archbishop a few days later prevented him from playing at the countess's palace; the emperor had been present, and the performers were each paid fifty ducats (or 225 gulden), half Mozart's entire annual salary in Salzburg.

He was beginning to get acquainted with Viennese musical life. He was friendly with the elderly court Kapellmeister Giuseppe Bonno, and had preliminary discussions with the actor and playwright Gottlieb Stephanie about an opera libretto. However, the archbishop instructed him to leave Vienna and return to Salzburg before the end of April. Mozart prevaricated, and in early May moved from his lodgings to take a room in the apartment rented by the Weber family. The entire Weber household had migrated to Vienna in 1779, following Aloisia's appointment to the German opera company. Fridolin Weber died that same autumn, and on 31 October 1780 Aloisia had married Joseph Lange. Lange was one of the highest-paid and popular actors on the stage in Vienna. He specialized in romantic leading roles such as Hamlet, and was also a talented painter. His first wife had died in 1779, and Aloisia was already pregnant when the couple were married. They set up an independent establishment, so in 1781 the Weber household consisted only of the widow Caecilia, the eldest daughter Josepha, Constanze and the young Sophie.

The combination of Mozart's disobedience to the archbishop, refusal to return to Salzburg, and lodging with the despised Webers must have been enough to send Leopold into apoplexy. Perhaps it is fortunate that his letters to his son have not been preserved, but we can gather the tone from Wolfgang's replies:

> I could hardly have supposed otherwise than that in the heat of the moment you would have written such a letter as I have been obliged to read ... I do not know how to begin this letter, my dearest father, for I have not yet recovered from my astonishment and shall never be able to do so if you continue to think and to write as you do. I must confess that there is not a single touch in your letter by which I recognize my father!

Mozart had a stormy interview with the archbishop in which he allowed his pride to overcome his discretion. According to a letter to Leopold, the archbishop

> Rushed full steam ahead, without pausing for breath – I was the most dissolute fellow he knew – no one served him so badly as I did – I had better leave today [and return to Salzburg] or else he would write home and have my salary stopped. I couldn't get a word in edgeways, for he

blazed away like a fire ... He ... called me a scoundrel, a rascal, a vagabond. Oh, I really cannot tell you all he said. At last my blood began to boil, I could no longer contain myself and I said, 'So your Grace is not satisfied with me?' 'What, you dare to threaten me – you scoundrel? There is the door! Look out, for I will have nothing more to do with such a miserable wretch.' At last I said: 'Nor I with you!' 'Well, be off!' When leaving the room, I said, 'This is final. You shall have it tomorrow in writing.'

His dealings with the Salzburg establishment continued for another month, until his celebrated interview with the chamberlain, Count Arco, who finally dismissed him with a kick on his behind.

In truth, Mozart's position in Vienna was fragile. He was not really sacked by the archbishop, but had resigned. Moreover, although the early signs in Vienna were positive, little substantial work had yet materialized. It is possible that he had already formed an attachment to Constanze, and that this was another factor that induced him to stay. He was certainly bitterly disappointed by the lack of support and encouragement from Leopold: 'In view of the original cause of my leaving (which you know well), no father would dream of being angry with his son; on the contrary, he would be angry if his son had not left.'

It is not surprising that this turmoil prevented him from concentrating on composition. The year 1781 was a slender one for music, although in the summer he completed a set of six sonatas for piano and violin (K296 and K376–80), that were soon published. These are fine works, quite different from the earlier sonatas in being genuine duos in which the two instruments have equal importance. They were published with a dedication to Josepha von Auernhammer, one of his pupils and a talented performer in her own right. The glorious Sonata for two Pianos (K448), one of the most joyous of all his works, was also written with Josepha in mind, and they performed it together in the autumn.

Nevertheless he was extremely poor during this year, despite the support of several patrons. Countess Thun continued to show favour. A second important patron was the Countess Marie Rumbeke, only a year older than Mozart, and his first pupil in Vienna. Her cousin was Count Johann Philipp Cobenzl, vice-chancellor and minister of state, and a distinguished politician. More than once, Mozart stayed at the Cobenzl country estate near Grinzing where he enjoyed the beautiful forest surroundings. The third important supporter at this time was Baron Gottfried van Swieten. Van Swieten was the son of Empress Maria Theresa's physician, and had been in the diplomatic service for a number of years. In 1781, he had just become president of the Commission for Education and Censorship, and from this position helped to implement many enlightened reforms. More importantly for Mozart, he was a connoisseur of music, and passionately interested in the 'archaic' music of J. S. Bach and Handel. He later wrote the texts of Haydn's two oratorios *The Creation* and *The Seasons*, and the was the dedicatee of Beethoven's First Symphony.

Mozart spent the summer in Vienna, smarting from his conflict with Salzburg, but confident in his prospects. Unfortunately, a fresh source of conflict arose with Leopold. Rumours reached Salzburg that his son was involved romantically with Constanze Weber. Wolfgang responded with a series of patent falsehoods:

> Because I am living with them, therefore I am going to marry the daughter ... If ever there was a time when I thought less of getting married, it is most certainly now! ... We went to the Prater a few times, but the mother came too, and, as I was in the house, I could not refuse to accompany them ... I will not say that, living in the same house with the Mademoiselle to whom people have already married me, I am ill-bred and do not speak to her; but I am not in love with her. I fool about and have fun with her when time permits ... and – that is all.

The Seraglio: 'I am so delighted at having to compose this opera'

At last in early August, some definite work came along from the German opera company in the form of a Singspiel (opera with spoken text). Mozart was given the libretto of *Die Entführung aus dem Serail* (*The Seraglio*) which had been prepared by Gottlieb Stephanie from a text by the Leipzig playwright Christoph Bretzner. Stephanie had recently been put in charge of the company and was a genuine theatrical craftsman, although widely disliked on a personal level. A visit to Vienna had been mooted by the Grand Duke Paul of Russia, following the alliance between the Habsburgs and Catherine the Great. The duke was expected in less than two months, and Stephanie no doubt already knew that Mozart could work quickly. A good cast was recruited, with the soprano role of Constanze being taken by Caterina Cavalieri, a popular and virtuosic singer who was said to be Salieri's mistress. The tenor role of Belmonte was played by Valentin Adamberger, the highest-paid member of the company and a fine musician, while Osmin was intended for the resonant voice of Ludwig Fischer, perhaps the best bass in Germany.

Silhouette of Valentin Adamberger by H. Löschenkohl, 1785.

Mozart set to work with a will, and before the end of the month he had written the Overture and much of Act I. In one day alone, he composed an aria for Belmonte, one for Constanze, and the closing trio of Act I. The pressure to work quickly was somewhat relieved when the Russian visit was delayed for two months. The project then received a further setback when the authorities decided it would be more seemly for the distinguished visitors to hear some opera seria before being regaled with Mozart's Singspiel. Two of Gluck's works were revived, and they were so popular that *The Seraglio* was postponed yet again. This must have been frustrating for the young composer, but it did provide the opportunity for quite extensive revisions of the original plan.

His situation was slowly becoming more settled. There was a touching episode on his name day (St Wolfgang's feast day) of 31 October. Mozart had recently completed a serenade for a six-instrument wind band of two clarinets, two horns and two bassoons (K375). This type of *Harmoniemusik* was very popular in Vienna, and was often played out of doors or as an accompaniment to social occasions. Just as Mozart was undressing that evening, the wind band placed themselves in the courtyard of the house

Muzio Clementi, engraved by Johann Neidl after Thomas Hardy.

in which he was lodging, and proceeded to serenade the composer with his own music. Two months later, he was involved in an event that brought him into considerable prominence. The piano virtuoso Muzio Clementi had arrived in Vienna as part of a highly successful European tour. On Christmas Eve 1781, he and Mozart were invited to a keyboard tournament at the royal palace in the presence of the emperor and the Russian visitors. Each played his own compositions, performed sonatas by Paisiello at sight, and improvised. Mozart evidently came off well, and was rewarded with fifty ducats (225 gulden). Even a year later, the emperor continued to talk enthusiastically about the event. Mozart was not impressed by the Italian virtuoso, admiring his technique but regarding him as a *mechanicus*. Clementi on the other hand said of Mozart's playing: 'Until then I had never heard anyone perform with such spirit and grace. I was particularly astonished by an *adagio* and some of his extemporized variations.'

Constanze: 'I love her and she loves me with all her heart'

The promising signs in Vienna at last emboldened Mozart to admit to his father that he was in love with Constanze Weber. In a letter calculated to appeal to Leopold's unsentimental and suspicious nature, Mozart emphasized how he needed order and practical assistance in his life, and outlined the financial advantages that would come from having a wife to take on some of the duties he otherwise paid for. He then described Constanze:

> She is not ugly, but at the same time far from beautiful. Her whole beauty consists in two little black eyes and a pretty figure. She has no wit, but she has enough common sense to enable her to fulfil her duties as a wife and mother ... She understands housekeeping and has the kindest heart in the world ... Tell me whether I could wish myself a better wife?

Leopold was predictably outraged. His state of mind was not relieved when Mozart was forced to admit that because rumours of intimacy had circulated in Vienna, he had been compelled by Constanze's mother and her guardian to sign a promissory document. This stated that he bound himself to marry Constanze within three years, and if he did not do so he would pay her an annual pension for the rest of her life. Although Constanze tore up the document, the damage was done. Leopold raged, feeling that his son had been manoeuvred into marriage by the unscrupulous mother, and even demanded that Madame Weber and Constanze's guardian be prosecuted for prostitution. This was the crisis point in Mozart's relationship with his father.

Mozart's fortepiano, made by Anton Walter about 1780.

Leopold had seen his practical influence over Wolfgang disappear with the move to Vienna, and now his emotional influence was threatened. Faced with a choice, Mozart preferred the Webers to his father.

Posterity must be thankful for this decision, since it probably saved Mozart as an individual. What he experienced was the problem that has confronted many precociously talented people as they mature. The paradoxical early creative development and late emotional dependency on the childhood mentor is far from unusual. Many prodigies suffer periods of depression, disillusion and loss of confidence while realigning their lives as young adults. They typically only survive as creative talents if their original ties are replaced by supportive adult relationships with friends or future partners. Almost invariably, these adult relationships are resented by the childhood mentor. There are many biographies of exceptional young people who failed to make this transition, persisting in increasingly difficult and cantankerous associations with their mentors, or going out into the adult world with little sense of direction.

It is clear that despite the accusations flung by Leopold, his son found support and warmth in the Weber family that replaced the security of

Mozart's marriage contract dated 3 August 1782.

his youth. Madame Weber's situation was difficult, with no husband and three unmarried daughters without dowries. Over the years, Mozart established and maintained good relationships with all the Webers. Madame Weber assisted the couple with their children, Mozart travelled with the violinist Franz Hofer who became the husband of the eldest daughter Josepha, and he worked professionally both with Josepha and Aloisia. Joseph Lange was a good friend, and the youngest sister Sophie attended the composer on his death-bed. Most importantly, in Constanze he found domestic companionship and affection.

Until recently, writers about Mozart have treated Constanze with the greatest hostility. Even the Mozart scholar Alfred Einstein was dismissive in a set of comments that perhaps say more about the author's view of marriage and relationships between the sexes than about anything else:

> She was wholly uneducated, and had no sense of the fitness of things … She was not even a good housewife. She never looked ahead, and instead of making her husband's life and work easier by providing him with external comforts she thoughtlessly shared the bohemianism of his way of living.

There is no evidence from contemporary records that Constanze was thoughtless or feckless, and later acquaintances such as the English publisher Vincent Novello described her as 'completely well-bred'. All Mozart's surviving letters that concern love and other personal feelings are directed towards Constanze, and express a sustained tenderness. There was a strong sexual element in their relationship, as well as close companionship. When he was away from her, Mozart became lonely and despondent, as on his concert tour to Frankfurt in 1790:

> I am as excited as a child at the thought of seeing you again. If people could see into my heart, I should almost feel ashamed. To me, everything is cold – cold as ice. Perhaps if you were with me I might possibly take more pleasure in the kindness of those I meet here. But, as it is, everything

seems so empty ... While I was writing the last page, tear after tear fell on the paper. But I must cheer up – catch! – an astonishing number of kisses are flying about – the deuce! – I see a whole crowd of them!

The new year brought opportunities to extend his concert work in Vienna. In February 1782, he described his daily routine to his sister Nannerl:

My hair is always done by six o'clock in the morning and by seven I am fully dressed. I then compose until nine. From nine to one I give lessons. Then I lunch, unless I am invited to some house where they lunch at two or even three o'clock, as, for example, today and tomorrow at Countess Zichy's and Countess Thun's. I can never work before five or six o'clock in the evening, and even then I am often prevented by a concert. If I am not prevented, I compose until nine. I then go to my dear Constanze ... At half past ten or eleven I come home ... It is my custom to compose a little before going to bed. I often go on writing until one – and I am up again at six.

His performances during the Lent season culminated in a concert he mounted for his own benefit at the Burgtheater in early March. A concert of this kind was put on by an artist at his or her own expense, and could be very remunerative if the audience was large. The concert included extracts from *Idomeneo* and the Piano Concerto in D major (K175) that he had written in Salzburg as long ago as 1773. He shrewdly gauged that the Viennese might prefer a more sparkling finale to the concerto, so he wrote a new Rondo with Variations (K382) as a replacement [CD 2]. Later in the summer, he joined forces with an impresario to give a concert in Augarten at which his Concerto for two Pianos (K365) was played, together with a Salzburg symphony. This was well attended by the nobility, so his reputation continued to grow.

The time for the production of *The Seraglio* came round at last, albeit at the theatrically unfashionable time of mid-July. According to Mozart, it faced a cabal and hissing from the audience, but triumphed nevertheless. The receipts for the first two nights alone were 1,200 gulden, and his own fee was 100 ducats (450 gulden). The opera was repeated eleven times in 1782, and continued in the repertoire for many years. It also travelled well, and by the end of 1783 had been heard in Prague, Warsaw,

The first page of the autograph manuscript of Mozart's 'Dissonance' Quartet (String Quartet in C major K465), one of the six quartets dedicated to Joseph Haydn.

Bonn, Frankfurt and Leipzig. It was of great importance in establishing Mozart's reputation in Germany, although in other parts of the world it has often been dismissed as attractive but slight. *The Seraglio* has unique qualities, with a brilliance of scoring and sheer beauty of sound that are unrivalled. The complexity of emotions expressed by the two pairs of lovers in the Act II finale are set with exquisite dramatic timing, and look forward to the subtlety of the great Italian operas of later years.

The composer proudly sent his father the original score and libretto in late July, pleading once again for permission to marry. But Leopold was unrelenting, and wounded his son deeply by his cool response to the opera. Mozart replied in great distress:

> I received today your letter of the 26th, but a cold, indifferent letter, such as I could never have expected in reply to my news of the good reception of my opera. I thought (judging by my own feelings) that you would hardly

be able to open the parcel for excitement and eagerness to see your son's work, which, far from merely pleasing, is making such a sensation in Vienna that people refuse to hear anything else, so that the theatre is always packed ... But you – have not had the time.

He decided therefore to go ahead and marry Constanze in a small ceremony at St Stephen's Cathedral; Leopold's consent arrived a couple of days later.

No paid appointment in Vienna: 'I cannot afford to wait indefinitely'

Mozart spent the next few months hoping to be given an appointment in Vienna by the emperor. His aristocratic patrons were in favour, and even the lordly Prince Kaunitz was said to have remarked, 'Such people only come into the world once in a hundred years and must not be driven out of Germany, particularly when we are fortunate enough to have them in the capital.' Mozart became increasingly frustrated, openly discussed the possibility of travelling to Paris, and even began English lessons. At the same time, he was carefully planning his campaign for the next major concert season. In doing this, he was unwittingly creating a new type of musical career, outside the employ of court or church. He reckoned that he could prosper by teaching, earning money from concerts, and by selling his music. The piano concerto was becoming a popular genre in which he was unrivalled. For the spring season of 1783, he therefore wrote the first three of his great series of Viennese concertos: K414 in A major, 413 in F major and 415 in C major. These works were precisely targeted. Although intended for piano and orchestra, they could also be accompanied by a string quartet, opening up the market for domestic sales of the music. Their style was calculated to please a specific audience:

These concertos are a happy medium between what is too easy and what is too difficult; they are very brilliant, pleasing to the ear, and natural, without being vapid. There are passages here and there from which the connoisseurs alone can derive satisfaction; but these passages are written in such a way that the less learned cannot fail to be pleased, though without knowing why.

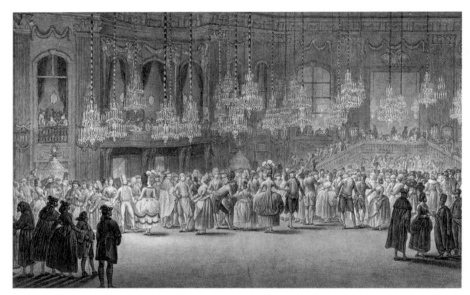

A masked ball in the large Redoutensaal, a chamber in the Hofburg palace used for public balls during the carnival season. Pen and wash, c. 1780.

He was active in other fields as well. On New Year's Eve 1782, he completed the wonderful G major String Quartet (K387), the first he had written for some ten years. A number of keyboard pieces in archaic Handelian style were written, perhaps at Gottfried van Swieten's behest, or because Constanze was fond of fugues. It is thought that the great Wind Serenade for thirteen instruments (K361) was composed around this time as well, possibly as a wedding gift for Constanze. Another work that Mozart began in her honour was the mighty C minor Mass (K427). The first (now known as the second) Horn Concerto (K417) dates from March 1783 and has the inscription 'Wolfgang Amadé Mozart has taken pity on Leutgeb, ass, ox, and fool'. This concerto and its successors were written for Joseph Leutgeb, a horn virtuoso and former member of the Salzburg orchestra, who had moved to Vienna where he supplemented his income as a cheese merchant. The scores are remarkable for the jocular insulting running commentary written by Mozart, and for the use of several different colours of ink. Mozart also needed symphonies for his concerts, so he asked Leopold to return the score of the 'Haffner' Symphony, a work he had hurriedly prepared the previous summer and sent to Salzburg for the celebration of the ennoblement of Sigmund Haffner. Leopold was uncooperative, and only sent the music after increasingly desperate reminders. The composer's response on looking through the score again is interesting: 'My new Haffner symphony has positively amazed me, for I had forgotten every single note of it. It must surely produce a good effect.'

Mozart is known to have performed in public concerts five times in 1783, not including his numerous unrecorded appearances in private gatherings. The most important occasion was his concert at the Burgtheater on Sunday 23 March, attended by the emperor himself and the cream of society. The programme was all his own music, and included the 'Haffner' Symphony, the Piano Concertos K415 and K175 (with its popular new finale), improvisations, solo piano variations, and arias sung by Aloisia Lange and the tenor Valentin Adamberger. An admiring notice in a Hamburg musical journal a few weeks later noted that the emperor stayed throughout, against his usual practice, and that the entire audience was unanimous in its applause.

Mozart and Constanze led a vigorous social life. In January they held a ball in their own lodgings that lasted from 6.0 p.m. until seven o'clock the next morning. Stephanie was there with his wife, as was Adamberger, Aloisia and Joseph Lange, and many other friends. Constanze was now pregnant, and the couple were enjoying life. In early May, he wrote to his father from the Prater:

> I simply cannot make up my mind to drive back into town so early. The weather is far too lovely and it is far too delightful in the Prater today. We have taken our lunch out of doors and shall stay on until eight or nine in the evening. My whole company consists of my little wife who is pregnant, and hers consists of her little husband, who is not pregnant, but fat and flourishing.

Joseph and Aloisia Lange. Engraving by Daniel Berger after Joseph Lange, 1785.

Constanze's pregnancy was in fact quite far advanced, and on 17 June their first child, Raimund Leopold, was born after a short labour.

Two more of the string quartets that were later included in the set of 'Haydn' Quartets were completed around this time. It is said that he was working on one of these – K421 in D minor – while Constanze was in labour in the next room. This anecdote has been used by commentators to illustrate the composer's emotional detachment. Even if the tale is true, it should be remembered that husbands were kept away from childbirth during this era, and that his behaviour was probably more of a stress-reducing displacement activity than a sign of insensitivity.

'I should dearly love to show what I can do in an Italian opera!'

The German national opera had not proved a popular success, and Joseph II had recently been impressed by the Italian troupe that Catherine the Great had brought from St Petersburg to a conference between the two monarchs. It was therefore decided to reinstate the Italian opera, and a company was formed under the supervision of Count Rosenberg, an Austrian diplomat whom Mozart had encountered during his Italian tour. It took up residence at the Burgtheater, and the German opera company moved to share the stage of the Kärntnerthor with the theatre company. Salieri was the musical director, and the poet was Lorenzo da Ponte (the librettist of *The Marriage of Figaro*, *Don Giovanni* and *Così fan tutte*), of whom more later. A fine cast was assembled, and the opera opened after Easter 1783 with a work by Salieri. In contrast to other major centres, opera buffa was greatly preferred in Vienna to opera seria. Vienna was consequently one of the few cities in which opera buffa was taken seriously, and developed beyond a superficial diversion into a major art form. Over the next few years, it attracted a number of opera composers such as Vincenzo Righini and the Spaniard Vicente Martín y Soler.

Mozart was desperate to write an Italian opera, and looked in vain through many libretti. Da Ponte promised him a text, but was much too busy adapting existing works. The composer therefore turned to his *Idomeneo* collaborator Varesco for a text. It was in fact to be nearly three years before a full-length opera buffa by Mozart was presented. However, he had an early opportunity to show his mettle with two arias and an ensemble that he prepared for insertion into a work by the Italian composer Pasquale Anfossi. These numbers were written specially for Aloisia Lange and Valentin Adamberger, and were designed to display them to best advantage. This practice of inserting arias that showed off the talents of specific performers was so widespread that such pieces became known as *arie di boule* (suitcase arias). Against convention, Mozart insisted that a notice be added to the libretto indicating that he had written the numbers 'so that honour may be given to whom it is due and so that the reputation and name of the most famous Neapolitan may not suffer in any way whatsoever'.

Varesco responded to Mozart's overtures by proposing the opera that was to become *L'Oca del Cairo* (*The Goose of Cairo*). It was perhaps this venture as much as his sense of filial duty that led the composer at last to make a long-proposed visit to Salzburg. It speaks volumes for the coolness that had entered his relationships with Leopold and Nannerl that neither side had made the effort to travel the 200 miles between Salzburg and Vienna over the past year. It also seems extraordinary to us now that Mozart and Constanze should leave their five-week-old baby in the care of a foster mother in a Viennese suburb. But it was just the two of them who travelled to Salzburg in late July, where Constanze finally met her husband's family.

Salzburg – for the last time

We do not know a great deal about the couple's three-month stay in Salzburg, and can only speculate on the emotional undercurrents. Outwardly, Mozart and Constanze appear to have taken up the familiar round of early mass, social visits during the day, games and music in the evening. Nannerl remained hostile to Constanze for the rest of her long life, although Leopold's sophistication would have prevented outright disharmony. It is certain that the atmosphere was charged; years later, Constanze recalled that on one occasion they were singing the great quartet from *Idomeneo*, in which the son sorrowfully says farewell to his father, when Mozart burst into tears and had to leave the room.

This was nevertheless a period of considerable musical activity. Mozart was hard at work with Varesco on the opera, although he eventually abandoned the rather absurd story after the basic plot became hopelessly enmeshed. He did, however, complete the charming Piano Sonata in A major (K331), with its opening movement in variation form, and famous rondo *alla turca*. The elegant Sonatas in F major (K332) and C major (K330) date from this period as well. He also helped Michael Haydn, who was hard pressed to complete a set of duos for violin and viola for the archbishop. Mozart wrote two of them in Haydn's own style, and no one suspected the deception.

Most important from the musical point of view was the C minor Mass. Mozart had planned the Mass even before he was married, possibly as a votive work in thanks for Constanze's recovery from an illness. The Mass therefore had special significance for him, and this may have been accentuated by the news in late August that his little son Raimund Leopold had died in Vienna, aged just two months. The Mass had remained unfinished since the previous year, and it was still incomplete when it was performed at St Peter's Abbey in Salzburg on 26 October [CD 2]. Constanze herself sang the florid soprano part, laying to rest the notion that she was not capable musically. According to Nannerl's diary the entire musical establishment of Salzburg was present. The couple left Salzburg the day after, and Mozart was never to return or to see his sister again.

Whatever the difficulties of this visit, there is little sign of tension in Mozart's subsequent letters to his father. They did not return to Vienna directly, but travelled by way of Linz. Here they were entertained by the elderly Count Johann Thun, father of no fewer than twenty-four children, one of whom was married to Mozart's Viennese patron, Countess Wilhelmine Thun. Five days later, Mozart gave a concert in Linz. Because he had no symphonies with him, he quickly composed the work that is now known as the 'Linz' Symphony (K425). It is difficult to believe that the symphony was not formed at least in his mind beforehand, since it is grand in design and quite belies the speed with which it was composed. It is typical of Mozart's genius that he combined an efficient and practical approach to music-making with an extraordinary breadth of imagination. They returned to Vienna at the end of 1783, and Mozart entered the period of his greatest popular success.

CHAPTER 10

Vienna 1784–6: Success, Freemasonry and *Figaro*

Mozart began a 'Thematic Catalogue' of his compositions in 1784. In this little book, now in the British Museum, he noted the date of completion, scoring and first few bars of almost all the music he wrote between 1784 and his death in 1791. Although scholars have questioned some of the dates, the catalogue is of immense value in charting the flow of his creative output. The year 1784 itself was a remarkable one, with no fewer than six great piano concertos, the exquisite Quintet for Piano and Wind (K452) [CD 1], the 'Hunt' Quartet (K458), the C minor Piano Sonata (K457) and the Violin Sonata in B flat (K454). The concertos were mainly intended for his own use, since during the Lent concert season he was involved in an extraordinary number of performances. His concert activity during March 1784 is summarized on page 101. This documents a rate of public appearance well beyond anything that would be tolerated by virtuosi of the modern age, none of whom of course write the music as well as perform it.

The title page of the Piano Sonatas K284 and K333, plus the Sonata for Piano and Violin K454, published by Torricella in July 1784. The edition is decorated with masonic symbols.

Mozart was engaged for five consecutive Thursday evenings to perform at the residence of the Russian ambassador Prince Galitzin, while he played every Monday and Friday for Count Johann Esterházy. In addition, he mounted a series of three public concerts of his own on consecutive Wednesdays. These were held at the Trattnerhof, a vast building on the Graben that had been constructed by the successful printer and paper merchant Johann von Trattner. Trattner's wife Therese was a pupil, and Trattner himself stood as godfather to three of Mozart's children. As well as shops and a concert hall, the Trattnerhof contained numerous apartments, and Mozart and Constanze moved into the building in January 1784. The concerts were attended by subscription,

Keyboard Performances in March 1784

Date	Venue	Date	Venue
1 March (Monday)	Count Esterházy (private)	17	Trattnerhof (public)
2		18	Galitzin
3		19	Esterházy
4	Prince Galitzin (private)	20	Count Zichy (private)
5	Esterházy	21	
6		22 (Monday)	Esterházy
7		23	Burgtheater (public)
8 (Monday)	Esterházy	24	Trattnerhof (public)
9		25	Galitzin
10		26	Esterházy
11	Galitzin	27	Trattnerhof (public)
12	Esterházy	28	
13		29 (Monday)	Esterházy
14		30	
15 (Monday)	Esterházy	31	Trattnerhof (public)
16		1 April	Burgtheater (public)

and people paid six gulden apiece for the entire series. Mozart proudly listed the 174 subscribers in a letter to Leopold, and it reads like a *Who's Who* of the Austrian, Bohemian and Hungarian aristocracy. It includes names such as Auersperg, Esterházy, Lichnowsky, Liechtenstein, Lobkowitz, Schwarzenberg, Thun and Waldstein, the famous Freemasons Ignaz von Born and Joseph von Sonnenfels, Nathan Arnstein the Jewish banker, Field Marshal Nádasdy and Generals Kollonitz and Nostitz, and the ambassadors from Russia, Spain, Portugal, Sardinia and Sweden, together with numerous court chancellors and other civil servants and merchants. The Concertos in E flat major (K449), B flat (K450) and D major (K451) were given at these concerts. The season culminated in

Extract from Mozart's list of subscribers, sent to his father in March 1784. It includes many of the most distinguished households of the Habsburg monarchy.

Mozart's own Burgtheater concert on 1 April, during which the Quintet for Piano and Wind was heard, together with a concerto, symphonies, and arias sung by Caterina Cavalieri and Valentin Adamberger (who had taken the roles of Constanze and Belmonte at the première of *The Seraglio*).

The piano concertos written during this period are strikingly different from earlier works, and Mozart was particularly proud of K450, 451, and 453 in G major. He sent copies to Salzburg in May, and was eager for the opinions of Leopold and Nannerl, since he realized that he was striking out in a new direction. The most dramatic change was in the use of the woodwind. Before this time, wind players had mainly been expected to reinforce the loud tutti sections of orchestral works, and therefore did not need to be very skilled. Mozart required all his wind players to be capable of solo work as well. The use of a larger orchestra

A busy scene in the Kohlmarkt, one of the principal shopping streets of Vienna, from an engraving by Carl Schütz, 1786. Artaria (third shop down) published many works by Mozart over the decade.

meant that it was no longer possible to perform these concertos with a piano and string quartet. This put the works beyond the reach of amateur players and small court orchestras. It is notable that very few of the concertos written after 1784 were published during the composer's lifetime.

Nevertheless, publishers competed to satisfy the public's interest in Mozart's other music. During this period, music was published either in durable engraved form, or as manuscript copies, and there were several publishers in Vienna using both forms. The most important publishers for Mozart were the firms of Artaria in the Kohlmarkt (then as now one of the most fashionable streets of the city), Torricella, and Franz Anton Hoffmeister, who was also a successful composer in his own right. The piano concertos written in 1782 and 1783 were soon made available in manuscript form, together with several sets of piano variations. In the summer of 1784, Torricella published a fine engraved edition of the Piano

Sonatas in B flat (K333) and D major (K284), along with the Violin Sonata K454. Artaria responded within weeks by publishing the three Piano Sonatas (K330–32), and other works followed later in the year.

Publication became an important source of income over these years. In addition, Mozart was probably paid for writing music for other virtuosi. The concertos K449 and 453 were written for his talented amateur pupil Barbara (Babette) Ployer, and in the summer he composed the B flat Concerto (K456) for the pianist Maria Theresia von Paradies. Paradies is celebrated not only for being a blind virtuoso (she learned new pieces with a complicated device involving wooden pegs), but also because she was the cause of Mesmer's humiliation and departure from Vienna. She was the daughter of a high-ranking official, and enjoyed a pension and special protection from the Empress Maria Theresa. Physicians agreed that her blindness had no organic cause, and Anton Mesmer took over her treatment in 1777. Soon afterwards, it was reported that she could see. However, her sight was fitful, and Mesmer's claim of a cure caused a furore and led to conflict with her influential family. Eventually Mesmer abandoned the treatment in disgust and left for Paris, arguing that she was persisting in her blindness to maintain her mystique and to promote her career.

Musically, the great excitement in Vienna in the summer of 1784 came with the arrival of the most popular Italian opera composer of the decade, Giovanni Paisiello. He had spent the last eight years at the court of Catherine the Great in St Petersburg, and stopped in Vienna to write a comic opera, *Il rè Teodoro*, while on his way back to Italy. It was a huge success and over the remainder of the decade, this and other works by Paisiello dominated the repertoire of the Burgtheater. His version of *The Barber of Seville* was particularly popular, and remained a favourite until it was superseded by Rossini's in the nineteenth century.

Mozart was on good terms with Paisiello, and in turn the Italian was impressed and indeed prescient about Mozart's music. When he was approached by a Rome impresario about whom to commission to write a new opera, Paisiello suggested Mozart, adding that 'he could not say for certain whether his music would please at first, being somewhat complicated; but that should Mozart once take, it would be all over with several masters in Europe'.

Unfortunately, during the first performance of *Il rè Teodoro*, Mozart fell ill with a high temperature, violent colic and vomiting. There has been much speculation about this illness, which may have been infectious, and some authors have suggested that his health began to decline afterwards. If so, there was little immediate sign. He was now extremely successful in Vienna and his annual income probably totalled several thousand gulden. His prosperity was such that in September he and Constanze left their apartment in the Trattnerhof for spacious quarters on the first floor of the Camesina House on the Grosse Schulerstrasse. The rent was 480 gulden per

The composer Giovanni Paisiello. Engraving after the portrait by Elisabeth Vigée-Lebrun.

year, in comparison with the previous rent of 150 gulden. The apartment (now a museum) was a stone's throw from St Stephen's Cathedral, and included six rooms, a kitchen, cellar, loft and sheds. It was here that a second son, Carl Thomas, was born on 21 September. In November, *The Seraglio* was given in Salzburg, and Leopold had the satisfaction of learning that even Archbishop Colloredo considered it to be 'not at all bad'. Then late in the year, Mozart took a step that was to provide him with spiritual support and an intellectual framework for the remainder of his life: he joined the Freemasons.

Mozart and Freemasonry

Freemasonry originated in Great Britain, but had spread widely through the continent by the middle of the eighteenth century. The movement made little progress in Vienna because of the opposition of Empress

Maria Theresa, but after her death there was a rapid expansion. By the time Mozart was initiated in December 1784, there were more than 700 Freemasons in the capital, organized into several lodges. The craft attracted a cross-section of society. About forty per cent of masons came from the nobility, another twenty per cent from the army, while more than twenty per cent were civil servants. Lodges had different characters and interests, and the lodge Zur Wohltätigkeit ('Beneficence') into which Mozart was first initiated had a reputation for charitable works.

Why did Mozart become a mason? Cynics have argued, then as now, that the main motive must have been social advancement. Caroline Pichler, the daughter of one of Mozart's bourgeois patrons, later recalled that: 'At that time, it was not unadvantageous to belong to this brotherhood, which had members in every circle and had known how to entice leaders, presidents and governors into its bosom. For there, one brother helped the other.' It is true that a large proportion of Mozart's patrons and his close musical associates were masons, including Baron van Swieten, Counts Cobenzl, Thun and Esterházy, Prince Lichnowsky, the publishers Artaria and Hoffmeister, and musicians such as Adamberger, Haydn and Cannabich. In later years, he also received financial support from fellow masons, particularly the merchant Michael Puchberg. However, I believe that the attractions of Freemasonry ran much deeper, and that the cult became important for Mozart for three main reasons.

First, masonry was based on the fundamental tenet that people should be judged on merit rather than birth or social position. Mozart had risen from humble origins to become a leading figure in European music, and wished to be evaluated on what he was, and not where he came from. He must have found the egalitarian atmosphere of the lodge very appealing, particularly after the bitter years spent in Salzburg in the inferior social rank of court musician. Secondly, masonic beliefs had much in common with the broader trend of Enlightenment thinking to which Mozart subscribed. A Viennese contemporary described the enlightened man as tolerant, eager for knowledge and self-improvement, a dutiful citizen and father, moderate and regular in habits. The true

Anonymous painting of a masonic lodge meeting in Vienna, c. 1786. Mozart is thought to be seated at the end of the row on the right, while a blindfolded candidate is being initiated in the centre of the scene.

mason was one who shunned self-interest and vanity in favour of fraternal sociability and integrity. There was a strong emphasis on coming to terms with death and its significance, and the ritual included statements such as 'The journey towards death is a journey towards our goal of perfection', and 'Be mindful of death, perhaps it is near at hand'. Mozart had been brought up as a Catholic, and his need for a supportive system of belief persisted into adult life. It seems to have been satisfied by masonic tenets.

   The third important attraction of Freemasonry may have been the ritual itself. Masonic ceremonies have a strong theatrical flavour, with special costumes and insignia, dramatic contrasts between dark and light, symbolic blows of the gavel, secret signing and ritual phrases. These features must have appealed to his dramatic instincts, since he was clearly inspired by the solemn proceedings to write some of his most atmospheric music.

He was admitted as an apprentice on 14 December 1784, and rapidly advanced to the rank of Master Mason. The lodge meetings were held weekly, and included initiation ceremonies, lectures on intellectual and scientific topics, and music. Mozart was soon involved in composition for masonic events. His first important work was the cantata *Die Maurerfreude*, written in April 1785 for the celebration of a scientific breakthrough in metallurgy by Ignaz von Born. Later that year, he wrote the *Masonic Funeral Music* (K477) following the death of two leading masons [CD 1]. He continued to write for masonic ceremonies throughout his life, and of course immortalized some of the rituals in *The Magic Flute*.

The title page of Mozart's cantata Die Maurerfreude *(K471).*

Leopold's visit to Vienna: 'For sheer delight tears came into my eyes'

The beginning of 1785 found Mozart busy working on two string quartets, the A major (K464) and the extraordinary 'Dissonance' Quartet in C major (K465). These two were added to four he had written since 1782 to form a set of six published later in the year with a dedication to Joseph Haydn. The dedication was fulsome in its praise of Haydn and is an unusual document. Mozart describes the quartets as being the fruit of 'a long and laborious study'. Dedications were generally used to please a patron, and were important weapons in the armoury of freelance musicians. The dedication to a fellow composer of such a major publication was therefore particularly touching.

It is not known exactly when Joseph Haydn and Mozart first met, but certainly Haydn attended two concerts in January and February 1785 at which the quartets were played as a set. The second of these concerts took place on Saturday 12 February, the day after Leopold Mozart arrived in Vienna for a three-month stay with his son. It was on this occasion that Haydn made his famous remark to Leopold that can be seen as vindicating the old man's life's work: 'Before God and as an honest man I tell you that your son is the greatest composer known to me either in person or by name. He has taste, and what is more, the most profound knowledge of composition.' Leopold arrived just as the concert season was entering full swing, and he was rapidly caught up in the activity. The day after the quartet party, Mozart played the Paradies concerto (K456) at a Burgtheater concert given by the soprano Luisa Laschi (a member of the Italian opera company). Leopold told his daughter that he 'had the great pleasure of hearing so clearly all the interplay of instruments that for sheer delight tears came into my eyes. When your brother left the platform the Emperor waved his hat and called out: Bravo, Mozart!'

Leopold left a detailed account of this period, from which it is clear that his son was as busy performing as in the previous year. There were many social engagements too. They dined with Frau Weber, where Leopold was surprised to find that 'the meal, which was neither too lavish nor too stingy, was cooked to perfection'. The day after they were guests of Gottlieb Stephanie, the librettist of *The Seraglio*. Although it was a Friday in Lent:

> Let me tell you at once that there was no thought of a fast-day. We were only offered meat dishes. A pheasant as an additional dish was served in cabbage and the rest was fit for a prince. Finally we had oysters, most delicious glacé fruits and (I must not forget to mention this) several bottles of champagne. I need hardly add that everywhere coffee is served.

There were additional dinners with Aloisia and Joseph Lange, and other actors, singers and friends. It is clear that during this period of his life, Mozart's social world was as vigorous as his musical activity.

Handbill advertising the Burg-theater concert at which the C major Piano Concerto was given.

As usual, he had written new piano concertos for the season. A concert in February saw the première of the dark D minor Concerto (K466), a work so dramatic and anguished in character that it must have bewildered audiences. Yet this was followed less than a month later with the graceful C major Concerto (K467) with its exuberant outer movements and serene Andante. In addition, he devised a cantata, *Davidde penitente*, from the unfinished C minor Mass, by altering the text and adding new arias for tenor and soprano. All this music-making took its toll on Leopold, who complained of constant activity, noise and late nights. After a month he admitted to his daughter: 'I feel rather out of it all. If only the concerts were over!' Nevertheless, he sent a favourable account of his five-month-old grandson, describing him as healthy and charming, and was also very positive about Constanze's economical housekeeping. He must therefore have been, for once, reasonably satisfied with his son's position.

'My beloved task – composition'

Popular accounts of Mozart's life suggest that he led a bohemian and feckless existence. This was almost certainly not the case. It is obvious that the intense rate of performing, teaching, composition and social activity described by Leopold could only have been managed by someone combining immense energy with rigid discipline. Mozart's daily routine in 1782 has been described earlier. Of course, this altered over the years, and the amount of teaching and concert work also varied across the seasons of the year. Nevertheless, it appears that composition was a task that had to be fitted around other activities, and in later years he often carried on into the small hours. The years of poring over manuscript paper took their toll, and by 1785 he is known to have used an upright desk so as to stand while composing.

Mozart worked efficiently, composing not according to whim but as circumstance (a concert, an arrangement with a publisher) dictated. He appeared to work out many of his compositions mentally before consigning them to paper, so many of his manuscripts have an exceptionally 'clean' appearance, with few corrections. There were occasions on which he did not even write out the music before performance. In April 1781 there was a concert at which he performed the Sonata for Piano and Violin (K379). He finished the piece the night before, so to save time wrote out the violin part and played the piano part from his head. Three years later, the twenty-year-old violin virtuoso Regina Strinasacchi visited Vienna and gave a concert at the Burgtheater. Mozart wrote the Violin Sonata K454 for her, finishing it at the last minute. They had no rehearsal, and once again he only wrote out the violin part, basing his own performance on shorthand notes.

This suggests that writing out the music was a late stage in the compositional process, and that many pieces did not require working out on paper. This impression was confirmed years later by Constanze, who told visiting English admirers how her husband used to wander around in an abstracted fashion while thinking about his music; then when he had settled the composition in his mind, he would ask his wife to chat to him while he set the music down on paper. His sister-in-law Sophie recalled:

> He was always good-humoured, but even at his most good-humoured, he was very pensive, looking one straight in the eye the while, pondering his answer to any question, whether it be gay or sad, and yet he seemed the while to be working away deep in thought at something quite different. Even when he was washing his hands when he rose in the morning, he walked up and down in the room the while, never standing still, tapped one heel against the other the while and was always deep in thought ...

Romantic commentators have concluded that because the physical act of writing was sometimes relatively mechanical, Mozart's music was God-given, and that he acted as some kind of 'divine conduit'. However, the impression is belied by the large number of fragments of composition that survive. Some are sketches of completed pieces, or manuscripts on which he worked out difficult sections. Other fragments are pieces that he never finished. Some of these were abandoned because they did not work out, but many were probably incomplete simply because they were never needed. Studies of watermarks and the stave ruling of the manuscript paper by the scholar Alan Tyson have provided a good idea about the time periods over which individual pieces were written. What has become clear from these studies is that the movements of many works were not all written at the same time. Some of the piano concertos have one movement dating from two or more years before others, while the Clarinet Concerto (completed in 1791) contains a movement probably composed a year before. It is tantalizing to think that if the occasion had ever arisen, some of the surviving fragments might also have been put to use as part of completed masterpieces.

The lasting impression about Mozart and composition is that he considered it to be his work. It was not something that could be left until inspiration struck, but was a practical activity that had specific purposes and a precise time-frame. If the music was not ready, did not suit the occasion or please the customer, so much the worse for the composer. In this sense, Mozart was part of the tradition of the Kapellmeister-composer, preparing music for religious festivals or court entertainments according to the requirements of employers. This is a far cry from the romantic view of the artist driven by inner conviction and heedless of popular taste.

Leopold, Nannerl and little Leopold

Three months after Leopold Mozart returned to Salzburg in late April 1785, his daughter Nannerl gave birth to her first child. Nannerl had married the year before at the age of thirty-three. Her husband, Johann Baptist von Berchtold, was a magistrate at St Gilgen, the town about six hours' drive from Salzburg from which Maria Anna Mozart had originally come. He had five children from a previous marriage, so Nannerl was faced with a substantial family even before her own pregnancy. She agreed to leave her new baby with her father, and return to St Gilgen without him. For the remainder of Leopold Mozart's life, the infant (who was christened after him) lived in Salzburg. This remarkable sacrifice of an only child to a beloved father is touching, but also has a pathetic side. Leopold did not tell Wolfgang about the arrangement, and was clearly hoping to repeat with his grandson the phenomenon of his own son's precocity. His reports back to Nannerl about the infant's development are full of wishful thinking:

> I can never look at the child's right hand without being moved. The most skilled pianist cannot place his hands so beautifully on the keyboard as he customarily holds his hand ... Often the fingers are placed with curved hand in the playing position, and when he sleeps his hands lie in such a way as though the fingers were really touching the clavier.

Nevertheless, it is not as if Leopold had dissociated himself from Wolfgang. On the contrary, his letters to Nannerl show how eager he was for any news from Vienna, however slight. He was particularly excited by a parcel that arrived in December 1785. This contained the six 'Haydn' Quartets in the Artaria edition (for which Mozart earned 100 ducats or 450 gulden), together with two piano concertos and one of the piano quartets. A few months later, he arranged a concert at which a pupil played the D minor Concerto, with Michael Haydn turning the pages. He was pleased to see the archbishop in the audience, together with all the dignitaries of the church and university.

It is also from Leopold's letter to Nannerl dated 11 November 1785 that we have one of the first indications of Mozart's new venture, a full-length opera buffa for the Burgtheater.

'He is up to the eyes in work at his opera *Le nozze di Figaro*'

Effective opera does not depend on the composer alone, but on the collaboration between the composer and librettist. As we have seen, Mozart was exacting in his demands on librettists, and remained dissatisfied by their responses. During the preparation of *The Seraglio*, he expressed his frustration to Leopold:

> Verses are indeed the most indispensable element for music – but rhymes – solely for the sake of rhyming – the most detrimental... The best thing of all is when a good composer, who understands the stage and is talented enough to make sound suggestions, meets an able poet, that true phoenix...

Burgtheater poster announcing the first performance of The Marriage of Figaro
on 1 May 1786. The title of the opera is given in both Italian and German.

Mozart met his true phoenix in the person of Lorenzo da Ponte, the
librettist of his three great Italian operas, *Le nozze di Figaro* (*The Marriage
of Figaro*), *Don Giovanni*, and *Così fan tutte*.

   Da Ponte seems in some ways to have been an unlikely person with
whom to have a successful collaboration. He was born in 1749 in the
Veneto, the son of a Jewish leather merchant who converted to Catholicism, and was educated for the priesthood. He was a promising scholar,
mastering Latin, Greek and Hebrew, and passionately devouring the
verse of Renaissance poets such as Ariosto and Petrarch. However, the
appeal of Venice was irresistible, and da Ponte as a young man flung
himself into the dissolute world of the city that lived by night. He had
several notorious affairs with married women, more than one illegitimate
child, and for a time lived in a brothel. He also developed a talent for
improvisatory and satirical verse, so was taken up by political factions in
the city. This led in 1779 to his downfall and banishment from the
Venetian Republic, and after a short period in Gorizia and Dresden he

arrived in Vienna in 1782. He had little to recommend him except a modest reputation as a poet and an introduction to Salieri. He had written no libretti or plays, and had only slight experience of the stage. Yet within a year he was poet to the Italian opera, adapting operas that had been written for other companies, and writing libretti and arias for the works presented at the Burgtheater.

It is doubtful that da Ponte held much appeal for Mozart as a person. The Irish tenor Michael Kelly recollected da Ponte as having

> A remarkably awkward gait, a habit of throwing himself (as he thought) into a graceful attitude, by putting his stick behind his back, and leaning on it; he also had a very peculiar, rather dandyish way of dressing; for in sooth, the Abbé stood mighty fine with himself, and had the character of a consummate coxcomb.

There were probably two reasons why da Ponte worked with Mozart so successfully. First of all, he shared Mozart's practical attitude to work. He did not regard his verse as sacrosanct, but realized that it had to be tailored and trimmed to suit the composer and the occasion. Secondly, his particular poetic talent was not originality, but a complete familiarity with verse forms, and an adroitness in adaptation. He was skilled at imitation and parody, and at fitting sentiments wittily and gracefully into precisely defined poetic modes. These were great advantages when adapting other stage works, as he did for *Figaro*.

Leopold Mozart was worried about his son choosing to write this opera, and one can see why. The play was infamous as a work of political satire. The French author Beaumarchais had completed it in about 1778, but it was not until 1784 that it reached the stage. It had been banned by Louis XVI, and had been submitted to the censors no fewer than six times. These problems were magnified in Austria, since Joseph II was somewhat puritanical in his theatrical taste. Beaumarchais had been imprisoned in Vienna in 1774 for calumny against the imperial family, and Schikaneder was forbidden to present a spoken translation of the play in 1785.

Much of the credit for convincing the authorities to permit *Figaro*

Lorenzo da Ponte, engraved after a portrait by Nathaniel Rogers.

must rest with da Ponte. He defused the text enough to evade the censor, while retaining a *frisson* of danger that would intrigue the audience. He was responsible for reducing the complicated plot to manageable operatic proportions, and for matching the number of important roles with the size of the opera company. The compositional task was complex, and Mozart wished to make no mistakes about his first opera for the Italian company. Thus it was not for another six months that the opera went into production.

Meanwhile, he continued his usual round of instrumental activities. In December 1785 he gave a series of three concerts for which he had 120 subscribers. The following year saw the printing of a calendar in Vienna containing silhouettes of notables, which included a portrait of the thirty-year-old composer. Three new concertos were written for this season, including the sombre C minor (K491), the E flat Concerto (K482) and the sublime A major Concerto (K488) [CD 3].

He was also involved in another operatic venture. In February 1786, Joseph II organized a party in the orangery at Schönbrunn in honour of his sister the Archduchess Marie Christine, the lively and intelligent governor of the Austrian Netherlands. The entertainment consisted of two short operas interspersed with scenes from well-known plays. The Italian company performed a piece by Salieri, and the German company gave Mozart's *Der Schauspieldirektor* (*The Impresario*). This must have been seen as a direct contest between the two traditions, and honours appear

The Marriage of Figaro:
*Scene from Act 1 as envisaged
by the French artist J.-P.-J. de
Saint-Quentin, and engraved in
the first edition of Beaumarchais'
play, published in 1785.*

to have been shared. Salieri had the advantage of the more popular Italian performers, while the Germans had Mozart's score. Mozart was paid fifty ducats (225 gulden) for his music, the same amount as was given to each of the singers for their one performance! Then, as now, opera singers were highly paid.

A few days later, Mozart went to a masked ball in the assembly rooms of the Hofburg Palace dressed as an Indian philosopher. Here he distributed a sheet of riddles and proverbs that he had written, entitled 'Selections from Zoroaster's Fragments'. Several of the riddles appear to have had vulgar connotations, but the proverbs include reworkings of well-known homilies such as 'I prefer an open vice to an equivocal virtue;

it shows me at least where I am', and 'It is not seemly for everybody to be modest; only great men are able to be so'. The whole episode seems to have combined his interests in the arcane and cryptic with his theatrical flair. Nevertheless, despite this exuberant level of activity, there are signs that Mozart's popularity as a virtuoso in Vienna was dwindling. His known public appearances as a soloist in 1786 were few. One reason may have been that from this year onwards, plays were allowed during Lent, so the scope for concerts was restricted. It was clearly the right time to move into the field of Italian opera.

'What is not allowed to be said these days, is sung'

Figaro was prepared for production in April 1786. Some music historians consider that the company working in Vienna from 1784 to 1786 was the greatest *buffo* ensemble ever to have existed. Not only were the individual performers outstanding, they had worked together for two years before *Figaro*. It was this experience that allowed them to cope with the new levels of complexity and subtle interchange that characterize Mozart's opera.

The linchpin of the opera buffa was the *primo buffo* or the leading bass-baritone. Vienna was fortunate to have the services of the finest singer-actor of his generation, Francesco Benucci. He was much sought after in Europe, and Joseph II rather ruefully admitted that three such singers would cost as much as 100 grenadiers. He was the obvious choice for the title role, and was later to play Leporello in the first Vienna production of *Don Giovanni*, and Guglielmo in the première of *Così fan tutte*.

The part of Susanna was taken by Nancy Storace. She was born in 1765 in London, the daughter of a Neapolitan bass player and an English mother, and was taken by her father to Italy at the age of thirteen. She was only eighteen when she joined the Burgtheater company, but had already appeared successfully in Naples, Florence, Milan and Venice. She was regarded as a lively and intelligent actress, and even the jaded Count Zinzendorf was ecstatic when she appeared, describing her as having a 'pretty face, a voluptuous fine bosom, beautiful eyes, a white neck, a fresh mouth, delicate skin, the naivety and petulance of youth, sings like an angel'. The Count and Countess were played by Stefano

Mandini and Luisa Laschi, two experienced and much admired Italian singers. The only native in the cast was Dorothea Bussani, the daughter of a professor at the military academy, who made her debut as Cherubino. She was married to the second buffo Francesco Bussani, and also created the role of Despina in *Così fan tutte*. She specialized in soubrette roles and was a vivacious performer.

Michael Kelly, the Irish tenor who was a member of the company, has left a touching account of a rehearsal of Act I:

> Mozart was on stage with his crimson pelisse and gold-laced cocked hat, giving the time of the music to the orchestra. Figaro's song, 'Non più andrai, farfallone amoroso', Benucci gave, with the greatest animation and power of voice. I was standing close to Mozart, who, *sotto voce*, was repeating, Bravo! Bravo! Benucci; and when Benucci came to the fine passage 'Cherubino, alla vittoria, alla gloria militar', which he gave out with stentorian lungs, the effect was electricity itself, for the whole of the performers on the stage, and those in the orchestra, as if actuated by one feeling of delight, vociferated Bravo! Bravo! Maestro, Viva, viva grande Mozart . . . The little man acknowledged, by repeated obeisances, his thanks for the distinguished mark of enthusiastic applause bestowed upon him.

Unfortunately, it appears that there were plots against a successful production of *Figaro*. The truth is difficult to discover now, since Mozart was always very sensitive to any hint of opposition. However, it does appear that the director of the theatre, Count Rosenberg, was ambivalent about the work, possibly because he saw it as a threat to his beloved Italians. Michael Kelly later recalled that Mozart was 'touchy as gunpowder', and that Salieri and his faction were responsible for these cabals.

The Marriage of Figaro eventually saw the light of day on 1 May 1786, an appropriate day given not only the content but the revolution wrought by this work on the world of opera [CD 2]. Its reception was rather mixed, since there was a strong claque in the gallery that interfered with the first performance. However, five numbers had to be repeated on the second performance, with even more on the third occasion. A few days later, Joseph II issued a decree forbidding repeats of any numbers apart from arias so as to stop the opera going on all night. A review in a

Viennese newspaper shrewdly recognized that this opera was so much more challenging than most, that it needed time and repeated hearing to be fully appreciated. Many of the audience may hardly have attended to the music, since they were intrigued about what the censor had permitted and were hoping for a politically inflammatory piece. Instead, they were confronted with a subtle and profound comedy of human relationships.

Travel plans

Soon after the première of *Figaro*, Mozart completed the second of his piano quartets. The first Quartet in G minor (K478) dates from the previous year, and a series of three was planned for publication by Hoffmeister. Over the next two months, it was joined by several other important chamber works, including the Piano Trio in G major (K496), the Trio for Piano, Clarinet and Viola (K498) and the 'Hoffmeister' String Quartet (K499). These were intended for publication and for performance by amateurs. However, Mozart's music was beginning to leave amateurs behind. A revealing discussion was published in a Weimar newspaper concerning the piano quartets:

> This product of Mozart's can in truth hardly bear listening to when it falls into mediocre amateurish hands and is negligently played. Now this is what happened innumerable times last winter; at nearly every place to which my travels led me and where I was taken to a concert, some young lady or pretentious middle-class *demoiselle*, or some other pert dilettante in a noisy gathering, came up with this printed *Quadro* and fancied that it would be enjoyed. But it could not please: everybody yawned with boredom over the incomprehensible *tintamarre* of four instruments which did not keep together for four bars on end ... What a difference when this much-advertised work of art is performed with the highest degree of accuracy by four skilled musicians who have studied it carefully, in a quiet room where the suspension of every note cannot escape the listening ear, and in the presence of only two or three attentive persons!

The second half of 1786 was dominated by domestic events. After a difficult pregnancy, Constanze gave birth to their third child on 18 October.

He was christened at St Stephen's Cathedral and Johann von Trattner stood godfather, but sadly the boy died just one month later. Living at close quarters with a sickly infant would take its toll on even the most robust individual, and only one work was completed during the child's short life.

Since Mozart was finding himself less in demand as a performer in Vienna than in previous years, his thoughts turned to foreign travel. Over the past months, he had acquired a small but important set of British friends. They included Michael Kelly with whom he played billiards, Nancy Storace and her brother Stephen (a moderately successful composer), and Thomas Attwood. Attwood was a protégé of the prince of Wales, and had been sent to study music on the continent. He had been Mozart's composition pupil since the summer of 1785. A large quantity of teaching material survives in the British Museum, including exercises set by Mozart and corrections in his hand of Attwood's efforts.

This English group was preparing to leave Vienna in late 1786, and encouraged Mozart to join them. His plans were apparently quite well-known, since in December they were even reported by a Hamburg newspaper. After learning that his father Leopold was looking after Nannerl's little boy, Mozart suggested that he leave his children in Salzburg while he and Constanze travelled through France to London. Leopold's response was scathing and unsympathetic, as he told his daughter:

> You can easily imagine that–I had to express myself very emphatically, as your brother actually suggested that I should take charge of his two children … Your brother heard … that the child [little Leopold] is living with me. I had never told your brother. So that is how the brilliant idea occurred to him or perhaps to his wife. Not at all a bad arrangement! They could go off and travel – they might even die – or remain in England – and I should have to run after them with the children.

In the event, these plans did not come to fruition because a new opportunity arose. *Figaro* had been presented in Prague in the autumn by a company led by an Italian impresario, Pasquale Bondini. It was a sensation and was repeated several times. Such was the enthusiasm that Mozart was invited by 'the orchestra and a company of distinguished connoisseurs and lovers of music' to come to the Bohemian capital to attend the opera. This was most unusual, and it is not known what sort of arrangement was really proposed. However, it was too pleasant an invitation to refuse, and shortly after the New Year he set off. He was accompanied by a large party including Constanze, their friend the clarinet virtuoso Anton Stadler, the violinist Franz Hofer (who was to marry Constanze's elder sister), another young violinist and her aunt, their faithful servant Joseph, and even their dog Gaukerl. This journey turned out to be the nearest thing to a holiday that Mozart ever enjoyed.

CHAPTER 11

The Darkening of Mozart's World: 1787–90

The party arrived in Prague on 11 January 1787, a couple of weeks before Mozart's thirty-first birthday. Immediately they were drawn into a dizzying whirl of entertainment, music and dancing. Mozart described their first evening in a letter to his young friend Gottfried von Jacquin, the son of a celebrated botanist:

> At six o'clock I drove with Count Canal to the … ball, where the cream of the beauties of Prague is wont to gather … I looked on … with the greatest pleasure while all these people flew about in sheer delight to the music of my 'Figaro', arranged for contredanses and German dances. For here they talk about nothing but 'Figaro'. Nothing is played, sung or whistled but 'Figaro'. No opera is drawing like 'Figaro'. Nothing, nothing but 'Figaro'. Certainly a great honour for me!

They spent several weeks in a relaxed fashion, playing music, visiting the sights and going to the opera. *Figaro* was of course performed, and on one occasion Mozart directed the opera himself. On 19 January, he gave a concert at the theatre, during which the 'Prague' Symphony (K504) was performed. This work marks a new phase in Mozart's symphonic style, with its high level of technical difficulty and chromaticism coupled with a brilliant use of wind instruments and comic opera buffa style. The

Count Nostitz's theatre in Prague, where Don Giovanni *was presented in 1787: drawing by Vincenz Marstadt, c. 1830.*

concert was successful, but Mozart must have been even more pleased to secure a commission to write a new opera for the autumn season.

Soon after their return to Vienna in February, Mozart participated in the farewell concert given by Nancy Storace. He wrote the wonderful *scena* for soprano, piano and orchestra 'Ch'io mi scordi di te' (K505) for this concert, and played the piano part himself. A few days later, the Storace party, which included her brother, mother, Thomas Attwood and Michael Kelly, arrived in Salzburg in two carriages each drawn by four horses. Leopold Mozart showed them around the city, and Nancy sang for the archbishop before they continued on their journey. She never returned to Vienna, even though Joseph II offered her the enormous salary of 4,500 gulden to tempt her back.

Apart from this concert, there is no record of any other public keyboard performance by Mozart during the 1787 season. For the first time since moving to Vienna, he did not mount a Burgtheater concert for his own benefit. There were a number of concerts at which his orchestral works were heard, put on by friends such as the Mannheim oboist Friedrich Ramm and the bass Ludwig Fischer. But it seems that he was not able or could not risk putting on a Burgtheater concert. The prophecy made by the Salzburg official at the time of his resignation from service had an element of truth: 'A man's reputation here lasts a very short time. At first, it is true, you are overwhelmed with praises and make a great deal of money into the bargain – but how long does that last? After a few months the Viennese want something new.'

This downturn in fortunes was signalled in April when Mozart and Constanze left their large apartment for more modest accommodation in the Landstrasse suburb of Vienna. This was a very significant change. In Mozart's time, the inner city of Vienna was surrounded by walls and a wide empty glacis designed to prevent invaders from approaching under cover. This is now the site of the present-day Ringstrasse, and the suburbs were built well beyond. There was immense snobbery about residence, and it was everyone's ambition to live in the inner city and not in the

A view of the Landstrasse suburb of Vienna engraved by Joseph Ziegler. Mozart and Constanze moved here in 1787 when they could no longer afford their lodgings in the inner city.

suburbs. As a contemporary said, 'Everything that is important, grand, noble, and wealthy finds its way into the city.' Travel between the two was expensive, since Vienna was so dusty that a carriage was essential for any visits or business involving the nobility, and this cost three gulden per day. An artist like Mozart was reliant on the patronage of the rich, and his livelihood depended on taking pupils and performing to the nobility. Over the next couple of years, Mozart and Constanze were forced to retreat to the suburbs over the summer and autumn, returning to the inner city for the season.

'Death ... is the true goal of our existence'

Late in March 1787 Leopold Mozart fell ill, and his daughter left her family in St Gilgen to come and nurse him. Mozart heard this distressing news a few days later, and sent his father a famous letter outlining his beliefs.

> As death, when we come to consider it closely, is the true goal of our existence, I have formed during the last few years such close relations with this best and truest friend of mankind, that his image is not only no longer terrifying to me, but is indeed very soothing and consoling! ... I never lie down at night without reflecting that – young as I am – I may not live to see another day.

It is known that Mozart was paraphrasing masonic writings in this passage, but there is no reason to suppose he was insincere. His contemporary and friend Count August Hatzfeld, a cleric and fine violinist, had recently died, so death was on his mind. He himself was probably quite seriously ill in April, although the cause of the problem is not known. Yet these events did not stop him from completing two of his greatest chamber works in April and May: the String Quintets in C major (K515) and G minor (K516). These were his first mature string quintets, with the two violins, viola and cello of a quartet being supplemented by a second viola, and he made full use of the richness of the inner voices. The other work completed in May was the splendid Piano Sonata for four hands in C major (K521), written for Gottfried von Jacquin's sister Franziska.

Leopold had apparently recovered sufficiently in May for Nannerl to return to her family. However, he relapsed and died on 28 May, probably of heart failure. We know distressingly little about his son's reaction to the death of a father who had been so dominant in his life. The letter he wrote to his sister a few days later betrays little emotion, but this may be because it was in response to a businesslike letter from her. There may well have been financial disagreements. Mozart's biographer Maynard Solomon has speculated that Leopold bequeathed the bulk of his estate to his daughter, leaving his son with only a proportion of the sale of his effects. This may have been a deliberate snub, or else a result of Leopold's impression from 1785 that his son was well off.

There are signs, however, that Mozart did not react to his father's death calmly. He had kept a pet starling since 1784 and it died a few days after Leopold. The composer buried the bird in the garden of their Landstrasse home, giving it the full panoply of a solemn mock funeral. A few days later, he composed the song 'Abendempfindung' ('Thoughts at Evening'), a meditation on the transience of life and the meaning of death for those who mourn. Perhaps his feelings were best expressed in this music. Leopold's life was summed up by their family friend, Father Dominicus (Hagenauer), the abbot of St Peter's monastery, as 'a man of much wit and sagacity, who would have been capable of rendering good service to the state even apart from music'. It is easy to forget that despite the strained periods in his relationship with Wolfgang, the two never broke off contact, and that the serious business was always leavened with humour and pertinent observation.

Don Giovanni

The Thematic Catalogue for the summer of 1787 is sparse. Only two works were completed, though both were masterpieces: the Sonata for Piano and Violin (K526) and *Eine kleine Nachtmusik*. This serenade was written for string quartet and double bass, although it is usually heard as an orchestral work, and remains deservedly popular for its perfect proportions and charming lyricism. However, the apparently slim output from these months was not because Mozart was depressed and inactive, but because he was working on his opera for Prague, *Don Giovanni*.

Don Giovanni, based on a seventeenth-century Spanish play, was in many ways an extraordinary choice of subject for Mozart and da Ponte. Here were two artists who had recently presented an opera on the most up-to-date risqué play in Europe, turning their attention to an over-used story that had degenerated to pantomime and street theatre. For many years, the Don Juan story had been the preserve of popular farce, far from the sophistication of the opera audience. A pantomime on the theme had been played regularly in Vienna on All Souls' Day, and there were several versions for puppets with grisly titles such as *Don Juan or the Quadruple Murderer*. Enlightenment critics were united in condemning the story for its tastelessness and irrationality.

Mozart in the house of Josepha Duschek in Prague.

What induced Mozart to select this piece? There was probably more than one reason. First, although the story was hackneyed, it remained popular. This might not be enough for success in Vienna, but *Don Giovanni* was written for Prague, which in the late eighteenth century had a much less refined audience. The Bohemian nobility who had sufficient wealth spent their time in Vienna, leaving the Baroque palaces of Prague to decay. Many of the fashions of Europe bypassed Prague, for as a contemporary English visitor noted, 'Everything seems at least five centuries behind.' This was an audience that was musically appreciative but not intellectually so pretentious as to disdain the old story.

The second reason for choosing *Don Giovanni* was that da Ponte had a libretto from which to work. This was a one-act opera written by Giovanni Bertati, and set to music by an Italian composer in Venice earlier in the year. As da Ponte details in his memoirs, he was working simultaneously on *Don Giovanni*, an opera for Salieri and one for the Spanish composer Martín y Soler, sustained only by wine, snuff and coffee.

Surely the main impetus behind the composition of *Don Giovanni* was that Mozart was inspired by the story. He was certainly not above enjoying the burlesque and pantomime elements, but also managed to create something much more intense and significant. The key to the opera is the final confrontation between Don Giovanni and the 'stone guest', where he eschews repentance even in the face of divine justice. Unlike *Figaro*, where each act stands coherent and balanced within itself, the major strands of the music and plot in *Don Giovanni* are channelled towards this devastating climax. The resulting drive and focus mark *Don Giovanni* out from Mozart's other operas – less perfect, perhaps, but reaching greater heights of dramatic intensity. I believe this could only have been achieved by using a plot that was already well-known, so that the audience were aware of what the protagonist's fate would be. Without the final denouement, the opera would consist merely of a series of disreputable sexual adventures by a charming but ruthless braggart and liar. But played out in the shadow of the forthcoming end, Giovanni acquires a heroism and grandeur that transcends his sordid actions. His defiance of death and refusal to be cowed emerge as intensely moving, and an affirmation of the human spirit.

Mozart travelled to Prague at the beginning of October for the production, and stayed with his old friend the soprano Josepha Duschek, whom he had known for more than ten years. Rehearsals did not go smoothly, because the small company found the work difficult to prepare and stage, and the première was delayed. It was finally produced at the end of October, and was apparently greeted with great enthusiasm. Mozart was paid 450 gulden, and also received receipts from a benefit night.

He and Constanze returned to Vienna in mid-November, and soon afterwards moved back to an apartment in the inner city. The famous composer Glück had recently died, and at the beginning of December Mozart received the imperial appointment of *Kammermusicus*, or chamber musician. This was a sinecure with a salary of 800 gulden, and was a mark of Emperor Joseph's esteem. The obligations were few, except that Mozart was expected to compose dances for the court balls held each year in the assembly rooms at the palace. Although he was grudging about the small salary, it was about the same amount as Salieri received as conductor of the Italian opera, a job that involved a great deal of work. The appointment might have marked an upturn in Mozart's fortunes. Unfortunately, external circumstances intervened to add fresh difficulties to his life as an independent musician.

War and retrenchment

By the second half of the decade, there were clear signs that Joseph II's revolution had encountered insuperable difficulties in several parts of the monarchy. The vested interests that had been threatened by his reforms combined in a tide of opposition. The nobility was damaged by the land reforms, the common people objected to measures such as high taxes on alcohol, and the intelligentsia were disillusioned by a lack of support for the sciences, literature and the visual arts. There was open revolt in the Austrian Netherlands and in sections of Hungary, and the opposition took advantage of relaxed censorship to propagate their views in pamphlets. The Freemasons were perceived by the authorities as threatening to the establishment, and lodges were amalgamated and brought under government supervision. Additional problems arose in 1787 soon after Joseph had signed a mutual support treaty with Catherine the Great at a summit meeting in the Crimea. The Ottoman Empire declared war against Russia, and Austria entered the campaign in 1788 with an army of nearly a quarter of a million men.

These events had major effects on the economy, since imperial subsidy for superfluous activities was cut. The German opera company was disbanded (their final performance was appropriately *The Seraglio*), and singers such as Aloisia Lange and Caterina Cavalieri were brought into the Italian troupe. The Kärntnerthor theatre was closed in February 1788 for the next three years, and the Burgtheater thereafter housed both the Italian opera and the German theatre company. Many of the male aristocracy were mobilized and left Vienna for the front, so private entertainments were curtailed. The campaign of 1788 was dismal, with the Turks gaining the upper hand. The war was waged in the plague-ridden Balkans, and disease was widespread. It has been estimated that

Luigi Bassi, the first Don Giovanni.
Engraving by Médard Thoenert, 1787.

over the year more than 170,000 soldiers fell ill and 33,000 died.

Conventional concert work was thin during 1788. A more positive event was the performance of a cantata by C. P. E. Bach. This was mounted by a 'Society of Noblemen' organized by Gottfried van Swieten for the propagation of serious music from earlier in the century. Mozart had recently taken over the direction of this organization, and he conducted Bach's cantata both at the private theatre of Count Johann Esterházy and then at the Burgtheater. It is possible that his Piano Concerto in D major (K537) was performed as an interlude between the two halves of the cantata. This society was to provide Mozart with valuable work in the future, and his growing familiarity with earlier music led to a refinement of his own style.

Don Giovanni was presented at the Burgtheater by the Italian company in May 1788, probably at the instigation of Joseph II. The composer was paid a further fifty ducats (225 gulden), and made several alterations and additions to the score. The changes in personnel at the Italian opera meant that the soprano parts of Donna Anna and Donna Elvira were taken by the Germans Aloisia Lange and Caterina Cavalieri. The opera was given fifteen times over the year, and was published in vocal score before the end of May. Joseph II maintained a keen interest in the theatre even though he was with the troops, but was of the opinion that Mozart's music was too difficult for the singers.

'I am really in very great need'

Mozart's financial situation had always been fragile even in his most successful years. Until his imperial appointment as Kammermusicus he had drawn no salary, so his income depended on his own efforts. He lived by teaching, performing and composing on commission. Teaching was a seasonal activity, since many pupils only wanted lessons in the winter and spring. Demand for Mozart as a performer had, as we have seen, declined since the middle of the decade, while publishers were becoming less eager to buy his music. The problem was that the public was learning that his works were too difficult for amateurs. The publication of the piano quartets was unsuccessful, and in 1788 Mozart failed to obtain sufficient subscribers to publish three string quintets at his own expense. Consequently, although his income never ran completely dry, there were periods of acute shortage. Mostly these occurred over the summer months when work was hard to come by.

One of the most distressing periods was the summer of 1788. It is from this time that the first of Mozart's letters to Michael Puchberg survives. Puchberg was a merchant and fellow mason, and Mozart wrote many letters to him, most of which contained requests for money. In June, the composer had been obliged once again to move out into the suburbs, and around this time he wrote a letter to Puchberg asking for help in a dignified fashion, stressing the bond of mutual aid and comfort between Freemasons:

> Your true friendship and brotherly love emboldens me to ask a great favour of you ... I have now opened my *whole* heart to you in a manner which is of the utmost importance to me; that is, I have acted as a *true brother*. But it is only with a *true brother* that one can be perfectly frank.

Yet only a few days later, he was reduced to much more desperate pleas:

> I am very much distressed that your circumstances at the moment prevent you from assisting me as much as I could wish, for my position is so serious that I am unavoidably obliged to raise money somehow. But, good God, in whom can I confide? In no one but you, my best friend!

Then at the end of June, his six-month-old daughter Theresia died. Vienna was in turmoil because bakers were holding back sales of cheap bread; there were riots in the city. Mozart's fortunes declined still further, so that in July he sent an urgent message to Puchberg: 'Owing to great difficulties and complications my affairs have become so involved that it is of the utmost importance to raise some money on these two pawn-broker's tickets. In the name of our friendship I am implore you to do me this favour.'

One might imagine that composition would be far from his mind under these circumstances. Yet paradoxically, the summer of 1788 was a period of intensive creative activity, remarkable even by Mozart's standards. Between June and September he completed two piano trios, the delightful C major Piano Sonata (K545) and Violin Sonata K547 (both intended as teaching material), and other minor works such as patriotic songs, canons and vocal music. The first two movements of the Piano Concerto K595 were also probably composed at this time. Most important of all, the last three symphonies were completed in June, July and August. The least well-known of the trio is the Symphony in E flat (K543), but it is every bit as fine as its famous companions, the G minor Symphony (K550) and the C major 'Jupiter' Symphony (K551). They were probably written for concerts that Mozart was planning, since he never carried out such large undertakings for no practical purpose. Another possibility is that he intended them for publication, mindful of Artaria's issue of Haydn's six 'Paris' Symphonies in December 1787. With these symphonies Mozart completed the gradual transformation of the medium that had been wrought over the decade. Before this, symphonies were expected to be played with almost no rehearsal, often as overtures to more important music, or as noisy conclusions to concerts. Mozart's works can be placed within the highest ranks of human creation, mixing intensity with grace, and eliciting a powerful emotional response from the listener.

We also have the testimony of a Danish visitor to Mozart in the summer of 1788, describing an idyllic Sunday afternoon spent with the composer in his garden.

> In the afternoon, Jünger, Lange and Werner came to fetch me to go to Kapellmeister Mozart. There I had the happiest hour of music that has ever fallen to my lot. This small man and great master twice extemporized on a pedal pianoforte so wonderfully! so wonderfully! that I quite lost myself. He intertwined the most difficult passages with the most lovely

themes. – His wife cut quill-pens for the copyist, a pupil composed, a little boy aged four walked about in the garden and sang recitatives – in short, everything that surrounded this splendid man was musical!

The sheer physical effort of all these compositions is astonishing. That Mozart could transcend the difficulties of his situation and sadness of recent events not only to remain cheerful, but also to unleash a torrent of creative energy, implies an exceptional mental resilience. It makes one even more curious about what kind of person he was.

Photogravure after the silver-point drawing of Mozart made by Doris Stock in Dresden in 1789.

Mozart's appearance and character

The descriptions of the appearance of historical figures are all too often frustratingly vague. However, most reminiscences of Mozart agree on two basic facts: that he was cheerful and sociable to an extent that was sometimes embarrassingly extrovert, and that he was deeply concerned with his personal appearance and his social presentation. Michael Kelly described Mozart in the mid-1780s as follows:

> He was a remarkably small man, very thin and pale, with a profusion of fine fair hair, of which he was rather vain ... He always received me with kindness and hospitality. He was remarkably fond of punch, of which beverage I have seen him take copious drafts. He was also fond of billiards, and had an excellent billiard table in his house. Many and many a game have I played with him, but always came off second best.

Joseph Lange, the husband of Mozart's sister-in-law Aloisia, knew the composer well throughout this period. He recalled Mozart's flights of vulgarity, noting that he

A watercolour by Giuseppe Piattoli of a game of billiards. Mozart was fond of the game and owned a table himself.

occasionally made jests of a nature which one did not expect of him, indeed he deliberately forgot himself in his behaviour ... Either he intentionally concealed his inattention behind superficial frivolity, for reasons which could not be fathomed, or he took delight in throwing into sharp contrast the divine ideas of his music and these sudden outbursts of vulgar platitudes, and in giving himself pleasure by seeming to make fun of himself.

We know little of his tastes or activities other than music and convivial socializing. He is commonly thought to have been ill-informed and uninterested in other arts and sciences, but this is improbable. Freemasonry had strong intellectual interests, and lodge meetings frequently involved scientific discussions and demonstrations. His book collection included historical, philosophical and travel books along with plays and dramas. Constanze later recalled that he was capable of sketching, and he was fond of dancing. His linguistic ability was extensive. German was spoken on a day-to-day basis, but high society preferred French, while Italian was the language of the theatre.

He had learnt some Latin at an early age, and even had a smattering of English.

Mozart's love of finery was such that when Clementi met him for their keyboard tournament in 1781, he mistook Mozart for a senior chamberlain or court official. When he died in 1791, the inventory of his wardrobe included three overcoats (one with fur lining), a black suit, a frock coat in red, one in fashionable nankeen, one in white cotton and another in blue, together with a satin embroidered frock coat, numerous waistcoats, and three pairs of boots. This was not mere vanity, but a crucial element of his self-presentation and image. The late eighteenth century was a time of social flux, when the traditional divisions between classes were becoming eroded. Dress was a mark of affluence, and a fashionable costume was for Mozart a passport into a class of society to which his origins and status did not entitle him. He felt that an appearance of material prosperity was essential, since it maintained his credibility in wealthy circles. One of the major concerns in his letters to Puchberg was that news of his financial difficulties should remain secret and his social credit thus be kept intact. The nobility and other wealthy patrons would not respond in the same way if they perceived him as a needy, unsuccessful musician. The one reaction that Mozart disliked more than any other was condescension – he had had enough of that in Salzburg.

These outward appearances were accompanied by a robust and sanguine temperament. Over the last decade of his life, Mozart faced many disappointments and sorrows with equanimity. He was rarely downcast for more than a short time about his experiences; Constanze described him as *'toujours si gai'*. The masonic code encouraged this way of coping, but at root lay a fundamental confidence in his own musical ability and talent. Mozart never showed signs of doubting the quality of his work, even when it was unfavourably received. This inner conviction sustained him even when he was beset with other difficulties.

Mozart and Handel

There are few records of Mozart's activity during the autumn of 1788. *Don Giovanni* was presented a number of times at the Burgtheater, and his operas were gradually entering the repertoire in other parts of Germany. Over the year, *The Seraglio* and *Figaro* were given in Brunswick, Hildesheim, Lübeck, Graz, Leipzig, Carlsbad, Regensburg, Frankfurt and Berlin. In September, he completed the Divertimento K563. This is far removed from the entertaining divertimenti of his youth, since it is a six-movement string trio written with an assured mastery and immense emotional range, placing it among the greatest of his mature works. Then in November, his adaptation and orchestration of Handel's *Acis and Galatea* was performed by van Swieten's Society of Noblemen. This was the first of several Handel orchestrations, and the *Messiah* was presented in March 1789.

The work was useful for a number of reasons. It brought him a much-needed source of money during difficult times. It also helped maintain his position with an influential group of wealthy aristocrats, including Prince Lobkowitz, Prince Schwarzenberg and Count Johann Esterházy. Most importantly, it brought him into close contact with Handel's music. It is one matter to read the scores or play through the music of an earlier generation, but quite another to work on it intensively, modifying the orchestration, making arrangements of entire numbers and judging small details. He was asked to make these adaptations because Handel's continuo-based orchestrations were regarded as too spare for contemporary taste. His work predominantly involved adding wind parts (including clarinets), and reinforcing the lower sections. He was assisted during rehearsals by the young musician Joseph Weigl, who later recalled that

> Those who never saw Mozart play Handelian scores of sixteen or more staves with inimitable dexterity, and at the same time heard him sing and correct other singers' faults, do not know him thoroughly, for he was as great there as in his compositions. One always heard the whole orchestra.

It is not surprising that this intimacy with Handel made a profound impression, and was one of the stimuli towards the spare, polyphonic style of many of Mozart's late works. It may also have revived his interest in church music. Although no complete works were composed over these years, the evidence from manuscript paper studies indicates several fragments date from 1787 and 1788, suggesting that he was inspired to return to this field.

The north German tour: 'Then came the happiest of all moments for me. I found a letter from you.'

The opening of 1789 saw little change in Mozart's prospects. The family returned to live in the inner city, and he wrote more dances for the carnival season balls. But the Lent concert season brought little work that we know of, so he determined to try a new tack, and mount a major concert tour. This tour took him north through Bohemia to the states of Saxony and Prussia. He left Vienna in April 1789 in the company of Prince Carl Lichnowsky, a fellow mason and son-in-law of Countess Thun. They travelled by way of Prague to Dresden in only four days. Mozart immediately called on the amateur musician and librettist Johann Neumann, where he met his old acquaintance the soprano Josepha Duschek. At mass on the following day, he was introduced to the Directeur des Plaisirs of the elector of Saxony, and that same evening a chamber concert was held at his hotel. One day later, he played his Piano Concerto in D major (K537) at the palace, and was rewarded with a snuff box containing 100 ducats. Then a virtuoso tournament against another organist took place under the supervision of the Russian ambassador. Thus within a few days, he had managed to display his talents to most of the leading figures of the state, and to be richly rewarded; Leopold Mozart would have been proud.

Yet the composer himself was unhappy. This was the first time he had been away from Constanze during their seven years of marriage. In less than a week he wrote to her saying 'Today is the sixth day since I left you and by heaven! it seems a year.' His letters were full of endearments for her and their son Carl, and he was thrilled when he received a letter from her:

> When the opera was over we went home. Then came the happiest of all moments for me. I found a letter from you, that letter which I had longed

for so ardently, my darling, my beloved! ... I immediately went off in triumph to my room, kissed the letter countless times before breaking the seal, and then devoured it rather than read it. I stayed in my room a long time; for I could not read it or kiss it often enough.

The real goal of the tour was Berlin. Prussia was now ruled by King Frederick William II, the nephew of Frederick the Great. He was an enthusiastic patron of music and competent cellist, and supported a considerable musical establishment. Yet although Mozart's presence was eagerly anticipated, the visit did not go well. The blame for this must be laid primarily at Mozart's own door. He appeared to lack the tact and diplomacy needed to ensure success.

It is interesting to contrast his experience in Berlin with that of Dittersdorf, who visited Prussia around the same time. Dittersdorf was a model of discretion, and began by composing six new symphonies for Berlin. On reaching the city, he immediately became friendly with Jean Pierre Duport and Johann Reichardt, two leading figures of the musical establishment. This brought dividends, since with Reichardt's assistance he was able to mount a performance of his oratorio *Job*. The king allowed the court musicians, choir and the opera house to be used without charge, and the resulting concert was one of the largest of the decade, involving some 230 performers. Even after paying costs, Dittersdorf was left with a profit of 2,500 gulden.

Mozart's visit would seem to have been especially well timed, since *The Seraglio* was being presented in Berlin. However, unlike Dittersdorf, he composed no new works. Although he wrote a set of piano variations on a theme by Duport, he was unable to hide his contempt for the resident musicians. He spoke despairingly of Reichardt's directing of the choir, and was irritated by Duport's insistence on speaking French. Consequently, he was given no help, and did not hold a public concert in Berlin.

He also spent some time in Leipzig, a university town famed for its bookshops and coffee-houses and guaranteed to appeal to an urban intellectual. He was encouraged by his friends to risk mounting an orchestral concert at the Leipzig Gewandhaus. The programme was all his own work, and included two concertos (B flat major K456 and C major K503), the scena 'Ch'io mi scordi di te' sung by Josepha Duschek, and a symphony. This may have been the great C major Symphony (K551), but documentary evidence is missing. Mozart's report of the concert to Constanze was terse: 'From the point of view of applause and glory this concert was absolutely magnificent, but the profits were wretchedly meagre.' He returned home at the end of May with some money, but not as much as he had hoped. Nonetheless, he was in high spirits, particularly when he anticipated his reunion with Constanze:

> On June 1st I intend to sleep in Prague, and on the 4th – the 4th – with my darling little wife. Arrange your dear sweet nest very daintily, for my little fellow deserves it indeed, he has really behaved himself very well and is only longing to possess your sweetest ... Just picture to yourself that rascal; as I write he crawls onto the table and looks at me questioningly. I, however, box his ears properly – but the rogue is simply ... and now the knave burns only more fiercely and can hardly be restrained.

The concert tour was almost certainly a sensible move, since no virtuoso could hope to sustain a living without travelling, even in such a cosmopolitan city as Vienna. However, Mozart's works were really too difficult to be performed without preparation by musicians in the places he visited. He did not plan the itinerary carefully enough to guarantee success, while his sense of musical superiority prevented him from handling the psychological sensitivities of lesser talents with sufficient tact to win their co-operation.

'Good God! I would not wish my worst enemy in my present position'

Mozart composed no music of consequence during his two-month tour, and the following months were equally barren. He had apparently returned from Prussia with a commission to compose a set of string quartets for the king, and a series of piano sonatas for one of the princesses. He completed the first of the 'Prussian' Quartets (D major K575) in June, and a piano sonata in the same key one month later, but got no further. It had been several years since he had attempted a quartet, and there was the fresh complication of making the cello part prominent, since this was the king's instrument. In addition, he was moving away from the dense texture of the 'Haydn' Quartets towards a more transparent contrapuntal style that required careful calculation.

Another reason for his failure to complete the commission may have been illness. He himself was unwell in June or July, but then Constanze (who was six months pregnant) fell much more seriously ill. Mozart was in despair.

> Great God! I would not wish my worst enemy to be in my present position. And if you, most beloved friend and brother, forsake me, we are altogether lost, both my unfortunate and blameless self and my poor sick wife and child … I must mention that in spite of my wretched condition I decided to give subscription concerts at home in order to be able to meet at least my great and frequent expenses … But even this has failed. Unfortunately Fate is so much against me, *though only in Vienna*, that even when I want to, I cannot make any money. A fortnight ago I sent round a list for subscribers and so far the only name on it is the name of Baron van Swieten!

Constanze's problems persisted, so that in the middle of July they clearly felt that she would die.

> At the moment she is easier, and if she had not contracted bed-sores, which make her condition most wretched, she would be able to sleep. The only fear is that the bone may be affected. She is extraordinarily resigned and awaits recovery or death with true philosophic calm. My tears flow as I write.

The exact nature of her illness is not known, although the fact that they consulted a physician specializing in gynaecology suggests difficulties associated with her pregnancy. She was advised to take the waters at Baden, and spent August in this spa town a few hours' drive from Vienna.

Yet despite these setbacks, Mozart was not forgotten in Vienna. *Figaro* was revived at the Burgtheater in August 1789, and proved more successful than in its first run. It received eleven performances that year and a further fifteen in 1790. It is possible that now the scandal of its presentation had subsided, the Viennese audience began to appreciate it for what it was, and not what they hoped it might be. The new prima donna was

Adriana del Bene, known as La Ferrarese, an Italian soprano who had performed in Italy and London before arriving in Vienna. As was customary for prima donnas, she was not satisfied with the arias that had been written for Nancy Storace in the part of Susanna, so Mozart replaced both the great Act IV aria 'Deh vieni, non tardar', and the short aria during which Susanna dresses up Cherubino in Act II. He was not very impressed by her, and said of the Act II aria: 'The little aria, which I composed for Madame Ferrarese, ought I think, to be a success, provided she is able to sing it in an artless manner, which, however, I very much doubt.'

Da Ponte's reaction to La Ferrarese was quite different:

> There came a singer, who without having great pretensions to beauty, delighted me first of all for her voice; and thereafter, she showing great propensity toward me I ended by falling in love with her ... She had in truth great merit. Her voice was delicious, her method new, and marvellously affecting. She had no striking grace of figure. She was not the best actress conceivable. But with two most beautiful eyes, with very charming lips, few were the performances in which she did not prove infinitely pleasing.

His partiality for La Ferrarese sowed dissent in the Burgtheater troupe, since she was given a precedence that was not deserved by her talents. Yet the revival of *Figaro* proved so popular that Mozart was at last given another commission by the Italian opera, his first since 1785.

Così fan tutte: 'A miserable thing which lowers all women'

If *Don Giovanni* was a surprising choice for Mozart, *Così* proved even more controversial. The story involves two soldiers who test their fiancées by feigning to leave on a journey, only to return and woo them in disguise. It caused immediate offence, partly because of the nature of the test, and partly because the women succumb to the glamorous strangers. Richard Wagner disliked the story so much that it coloured his opinion of the music: 'Oh how doubly dear and above all honour is Mozart to me, that it was not possible for him to invent music ... for *Così* like that of *Figaro*! How shamefully would it have desecrated Music!' It was asserted by

The Burgtheater poster for the first production of Così fan tutte *in January 1790.*
The opera is also given its subtitle 'La scole degli amanti', or 'The School for Lovers'.

early biographers that Mozart was forced to compose the opera, perhaps even by the emperor himself, so could not refuse, and that the story was based on fact. It has also been mooted that the emphasis on women's frailty was a reflection on Mozart's own life.

However, none of these proposals is plausible. The story of *Così* is based on a set of themes that originated in classical times, and resurfaced in the works of Boccaccio, Shakespeare, Ariosto and Cervantes. It was just like da Ponte to use his knowledge of Renaissance literature in this fashion. Moreover, it is doubtful that the story had any personal significance for Mozart, since it was probably not even written for him. Evidence has recently been unearthed suggesting that the libretto was first intended for Salieri, and that only later was it transferred to Mozart.

What we do know is that Mozart took great care to match the music to his singers. La Ferrarese was given the role of Fiordiligi, a bravura part of great virtuosity. She was known for the extent of her vocal range and large leaps from top to bottom of the register, and Mozart exploited this in the role. Since her acting ability was limited, Mozart used the part to parody the static emotions of opera seria. The second soprano part was taken by Louise Villeneuve, and Mozart learned about her voice by writing two insertion arias for her in the autumn. Guglielmo was taken by the ever popular Benucci, and Despina by Dorothea Bussani (the first Cherubino). In the person of Vincenzo Calvesi, Mozart had his best tenor since Raaff, and the part of Ferrando was developed accordingly.

Così fan tutte: *title page of a piano score, Paris 1822.*

What Mozart achieved in *Così* was an ensemble opera. The tightly-knit symmetrical plot is coupled with an exceptionally integrated score containing many duets, trios and quartets. The arias are incorporated into the fabric of the story, instead of standing out as displays for their own sake. Musically, the work is unified by a characteristic sonority in instrumentation, an orderly progression of keys, and by thematic reminiscences across different stretches of the score. The emotional tone is ambivalent, generating a strong sense of parody and profound difficulty in distinguishing sincerity of expression from falsehood. It is a very sophisticated opera, and was designed specifically for the wealthy intellectual audience of the Burgtheater that Mozart knew so well.

In setting the tone for this opera, Mozart rightly perceived that his audience did not wish to be challenged by notions of social upheaval, but would prefer an amusing exposition of more personal human foibles. For above all, this was a period of increasing uncertainty. On the one hand, the fall of the Bastille in the summer had sent tremors through the royal courts of Europe, and rumours of revolution were widespread. In contrast, the war with Turkey had taken a more successful turn, with the capture of Belgrade in October and Bucharest in November. There were triumphant parades in Vienna, a special Te Deum was sung in the cathedral, and more than 100,000 people crowded the streets to applaud the sovereign.

We do not know how Mozart felt about these events. He spent most of the autumn preparing his opera. The one other substantial work to be completed during this period was the Clarinet Quintet (K581), for many people the most touching of all his chamber works, tinged with a melancholy beauty. It was written for his friend the clarinettist Anton Stadler for a concert of the Society of Musicians in December. In November, Constanze's difficult pregnancy came to an end, and a girl was born who did not survive the day.

The year 1789 was one of the leanest of Mozart's maturity in terms of substantial compositions. He had spent two months on a concert tour that had only been partly successful, had endured the worry of a summer of financial crisis and illness, and had the further sadness of a fourth child dying in infancy. On the larger scene, it became clear that the Emperor Joseph II, who had been a source of support and admiration, was dying. The months spent at the war front had taken their toll on his health. He responded to the political opposition and failure of his reforms by reversing his liberalism. Censorship became firmer, and there was a sinister increase in the power of the police. Joseph worked on with characteristic energy, but was not well enough to attend the première of *Così* on 26 January 1790. He died of tuberculosis on 20 February, and his great experiment in enlightened rule was over. It seems appropriate that Mozart's last Italian comic opera should coincide with this event, since his genius had flourished under Joseph's rule. As a contemporary newspaper reported a few weeks later: 'That the music is by Mozart says, I believe, everything.'

CHAPTER 12

The Last Years: New Directions, Revival and Death

Joseph II was succeeded by his brother Leopold, who entered Vienna on 13 March 1790. Leopold was grand duke of Tuscany, had lived in Florence for twenty-five years, and possessed a very different style. He had heartily disliked Joseph and was opposed to his policies, although on a smaller scale in Tuscany he had instituted many reforms in education, trade and the economy. His most immediate problem as ruler of the Habsburg realm was the war, for it was feared that Prussia would take up arms on the Turkish side. This was forestalled by Leopold's diplomacy, and peace was established in the summer.

Mozart suffered financially from the disruption of the concert season by the death of Joseph II. It is also possible that he received less money than he had hoped from the composition of *Così fan tutte*. Early in April he wrote to Puchberg requesting a loan, and his friend sent him 150 gulden. Yet only a week later, Mozart was desperate: 'If you can and will extricate me from a temporary embarrassment, then, for the love of God, do so! Whatever you can easily spare will be welcome. If possible, forget my importunity and forgive me.' He is known to have played in a chamber concert for a Hungarian aristocrat early in April, which included the String Trio (K563) and the Clarinet Quintet. Another concert was held in his own apartment when the newly completed String Quartet (K589) was played. Nevertheless, in early May he turned to Puchberg once again for help with a large haberdasher's bill, and he was obliged to approach money-lenders as well as his personal friends for support.

Mozart was hopeful that he would receive more substantial employment from the new emperor and his family. He drafted a petition to Archduke Francis, Leopold's son and heir, requesting that he be appointed second Kapellmeister to Salieri, 'particularly as Salieri, that very gifted

The Empress Maria Luisa and her husband Leopold who succeeded his brother Joseph II as emperor in 1790, bringing distinctly Italian musical tastes to Vienna. Engraved by Franz Heger.

Kapellmeister, has never devoted himself to church music, whereas from my youth up I have made myself completely familiar with this style'. It is not known whether the petition was sent, but certainly it came to nothing. One reason is that Leopold's succession led to substantial changes in Viennese cultural life. Leopold was steeped in Italian music; he had moved to Florence when he was eighteen, so his taste had been formed there. Musically, he is most famous for an occasion in February 1792, when he was so delighted by the opera *Il matrimonio segreto* which he had commissioned from Cimarosa, that he commanded that it be encored in its entirety. The new queen (shortly to become empress) was the Spanish Infanta Maria Luisa, who was said not to take 'any particular pleasure from our music in Vienna'. Mozart's prospects of advancement were therefore slim.

Nor was he the only one to suffer. For the past decade, Salieri had been Joseph II's favourite composer and had been the arbiter of musical activity in Vienna. With the support of his mentor Gluck, Salieri had triumphed on the operatic stage in Paris as well as Vienna. Leopold and his courtiers had wider Italian tastes, and in the autumn of 1790, Salieri petitioned to be released from his role as musical director of the opera. He continued in a reduced capacity, but many of his responsibilities devolved on Joseph Weigl, the deputy who had assisted Mozart in the rehearsals of *Figaro*, and had directed *Figaro*, *Don Giovanni* and probably *Così fan tutte* when Mozart was not present. Count Rosenberg was replaced as director of the court theatres, and da Ponte's position also became fragile.

Mozart composed little during the first half of 1790 except the third String Quartet (K590) for the king of Prussia. He was at work on two further Handel arrangements for van Swieten's Society, *Alexander's Feast* and the *Ode for St Cecilia's Day*. However, his health was not good, and he complained of head pains, toothache and fatigue. Constanze was also ill, and was prescribed sixty baths. She went once again to Baden, and on this occasion her husband probably stayed with her most of the time to save on expenses. Perhaps the lowest point of all was in August 1790, when Mozart wrote desperately to Puchberg:

> Whereas I felt tolerably well yesterday, I am absolutely wretched today. I could not sleep all night for pain. I must have got overheated yesterday from walking so much and then without knowing it have caught a chill. Picture to yourself my condition – ill and consumed by worries and anxieties. Such a state quite definitely prevents me from recovering. In a week or a fortnight I shall be better off – certainly – but at present I am in want! Can you not help me out with a trifle? The smallest sum would be very welcome just now.

Puchberg replied with the paltry sum of ten gulden.

Events later in the year provided further evidence that Mozart had little future with the Habsburg court. The wife of the Archduke Francis had died in childbirth in February, and by September a match had been arranged for him with Maria Theresa, the daughter of King Ferdinand and Queen Maria Carolina of Naples – the same royal couple who had given young Mozart such a lukewarm reception twenty years earlier. It was to be a double wedding, since the Archduke Ferdinand married another princess from Naples. These weddings were celebrated with pomp and ceremony, and Salieri, Haydn and Weigl were all involved. But Mozart was not called upon to produce any works, and was completely ignored.

The small but fashionable spa town of Baden, near Vienna, where Constanze stayed for her health on several occasions. Drawing by Lorenz Janscha, late eighteenth century.

The last tour: Frankfurt and the coronation

The accession of Leopold to the throne involved a number of different coronations for the various lands he ruled. The most important was his coronation as Holy Roman Emperor, which took place in the city of Frankfurt. This was an occasion of immense diplomatic importance, and princely and ecclesiastical dignitaries congregated in great numbers. Leopold's own retinue contained more than two and a half thousand soldiers, but he took only fifteen musicians led by Salieri. Mozart therefore decided to make the journey at his own expense, in the hope of capitalizing on the presence of so many potential patrons.

He set out on 28 September with Franz Hofer, now his brother-in-law, in his own carriage. Once again, he considered it essential to present himself as a successful musician, even though he had to pawn his plate to finance the journey. His first letter to Constanze brimmed with optimism: 'I am firmly resolved to make as much money as I can here and then return to you with great joy. What a glorious life we shall have then! I will work – work so hard – that no unforeseen accidents shall ever reduce us to such desperate straits again.' When he reached Frankfurt, he was fortunate to fall in with Johann Böhm, the theatre manager who had spent a season in Salzburg in 1779. During the coronation, visitors could expect to pay the enormous sum of ten gulden a day for a room in an inn, but Mozart made arrangements through Böhm for a lodging at only thirty gulden per month.

The coronation took place on 9 October, with music by Righini, formerly an operatic rival and now Kapellmeister in nearby Mainz. Böhm's company put on *The Seraglio* on the 12th, and then on Friday 15 October Mozart gave his own concert. He had not written any new works for the event, since he had accumulated plenty of music with which the audience would not be familiar. The programme included the Piano Concerto in F major (K459) and the D major 'Coronation' Concerto (K537), vocal music, improvisations and at least one symphony. Mozart's report of the concert to his wife was brief:

> My concert took place at eleven o'clock this morning. It was a splendid success from the point of view of honour and glory, but a failure as far as money was concerned. Unfortunately, some Prince was giving a big *déjeuner* and the Hessian troops were holding a grand manoeuvre. But in any case some obstacle has arisen on every day during my stay here.

An eye-witness account of his concert survives in the travel diaries of Count Bentheim-Steinfurt. He describes Mozart as a 'small man of rather pleasant appearance: He had a coat of brown marine satin nicely embroidered'. He was playing a fortepiano made by Stein, and during his charming improvisation 'he shone infinitely, exhibiting all the powers of his talent'. But the audience was small, the orchestra a meagre twenty players, and there were long pauses between the pieces. In the end, the concert was abandoned before the final symphony since everyone was ready for dinner.

The next day Mozart sailed down the Rhine to Mainz where the concert in all its essentials was repeated in the palace of the elector-archbishop. He received the equivalent of about 165 gulden from the court, and moved on to visit Mannheim for a couple of days. His short stay coincided with a performance of *Figaro*, and this was probably the first time he had heard it in a German translation. He returned to Vienna by way of Munich where he renewed his friendship with Cannabich, Ramm and others. It was here that he finally got to perform for King Ferdinand of Naples, since the royal party was staying in Munich on its way back from the coronation.

Mozart reached Vienna again in the second week of November. The tour cannot have been judged a financial success, although he was greatly admired in many of the cities he visited. In view of his death the following year, this brief circuit of the places in which he had been happy in his youth has taken on an elegiac quality for later biographers. But it is notable that he was not inclined to stop in Salzburg, or to visit his sister in St Gilgen. Interestingly, Mozart returned with a revival of energy and creative vitality. As in his youth, his exposure to the music and tastes of different centres stimulated him to fresh musical experiments.

A London offer

While Mozart was away in Frankfurt, Constanze had moved their household to a new apartment on the Rauhensteingasse in the inner city. The first-floor apartment was spacious although rather dark, and had four substantial rooms as well as a kitchen and services. The rent was 330 gulden per annum, greater than any others Mozart paid except during his heyday between 1784 and 1787. This suggests that the financial arrangements they had been negotiating over the past months had led to a more stable situation. Mozart was also willing, for one of the few times in his life, to compose commercial music for cash. The celebrated conqueror of Belgrade, Field Marshal Laudon, had died in the summer of 1790. His achievements were immortalized by an entrepreneur in a waxworks 'mausoleum' where every hour a mechanical barrel pipe organ played solemn funeral music. Mozart was induced to write his Adagio and Allegro (K594) for this instrument, followed by two other pieces in 1791. He evidently loathed the work:

> I compose a bit of it every day – but I have to break off now and then, as I get bored. And indeed I would give the whole thing up, if I had not such an important reason to go on with it ... If it were for a large instrument and the work would sound like an organ piece, then I might get some fun out of it. But, as it is, the work consists solely of little pipes which sound too high-pitched and too childish for my taste.

A far more interesting proposal greeted Mozart when he returned to Vienna. The manager of the King's Theatre at the Pantheon in London invited him to England for six months in order to write two operas. For this he was to be paid the enormous sum of £300, equivalent to some 3,000 Viennese gulden. The offer had probably been brokered by Nancy Storace, who was enjoying great success in London at the time. There has been much speculation about why he did not accept this attractive proposal. It was just around this time that the London-based impresario Salomon had engaged Haydn for the next season of his Hanover Square concerts. It seems unlikely that Leopold's court in Vienna held much attraction. But it is possible that he felt it would be inappropriate and disadvantageous for both him and Haydn to arrive in London for the same season, and that his own visit should be delayed. Another consideration was probably Constanze's health. She was pregnant yet again, and they must have discussed the difficulties she had experienced on earlier occasions.

Haydn left for London on 15 December, and the two men met for the last time at a dinner on the day before. Mozart had just completed his great String Quintet in D major (K593) [CD 3], and this was performed by an ensemble in which both men played. Haydn later recalled that Mozart was very emotional on this occasion and was convinced that they would never meet again. At the time, Haydn attributed this sentiment to concern about his relatively advanced age, not to any premonition by Mozart of an early death for himself.

The D major Quintet entered Mozart's Thematic Catalogue in

December, and over the next few months it was joined by many more pieces. This was the first carnival season during which he had a real opportunity to impress the court in his post as Kammermusicus, and the season was particularly lively because of the presence of the Neapolitan royal party. He therefore composed a great number of dances that proved very popular, and were soon on sale in manuscript copies. Mozart's last piano concerto, the sublime B flat major (K595), was completed in January. He probably began the work two years before, and it is thought to have been performed by his former pupil Babette Ployer early in 1791. Mozart himself played it at a benefit concert given by a visiting clarinet virtuoso in March – the first occasion on which he is known to have played a concerto in public in Vienna for five years. The following month, he completed his last string quintet (K614) for Johann Tost, a former violinist in Haydn's orchestra in Eszterháza who had married a wealthy woman and become a gentleman of leisure. This quintet has never been admired so much as its predecessors, since it is laid out in the style favoured by Haydn rather than the grand form of the Quintets in C, G minor and D major. Another important event in April was the traditional large Easter concert of the Society of Musicians, at which one of the late symphonies was performed. It is thought that the symphony in question was the great G minor (K550), given in a revised version that included clarinets. Altogether, it is clear that his music was heard in a wide variety of settings over these months.

Mozart appears to have been in debt once again in April, but he formulated a new plan to secure his future through the church. The Kapellmeister of St Stephen's Cathedral in Vienna was Leopold Hofmann, who was over sixty. Since he was not expected to continue much longer, Mozart petitioned the municipal council to be appointed assistant Kapellmeister without pay, on the understanding that he would take over from Hofmann in due course. He was no doubt aware that Hofmann was a rich man (his estate amounted to more than 18,000 gulden on his death in 1793). The petition was granted, and it is interesting to speculate about the directions Mozart's music might have taken had the plan come to fruition. There are signs that he was at work on church music at this time, although he was also composing a fourth horn concerto for his friend Joseph Leutgeb. The concerto (now paradoxically known as the first) was never finished, probably because Mozart became too busy with another major project – *The Magic Flute.*

The Magic Flute: A masonic Singspiel

Mozart's activities over the first months of 1791 suggest that he was moving outside the orbit of the court and aristocracy and turning towards

Aufsicht gegen die Vorstädte Vieden und Vien.   *Vüe vers les Faubourg nommé Vieden et Vien.*

A view towards the Wieden suburb of Vienna. In the centre is the Freihaus, containing the theatre at which The Magic Flute *was first performed in 1791.*

*Emanuel Schikaneder as
Papageno, engraved in 1791
by Ignaz Alberti.*

bourgeois patrons and audiences. This change
is nowhere more striking than in *The Magic Flute*,
which was written to a German text by Emanuel
Schikaneder, and performed not at the Burgtheater or the Kärntnerthor theatre, but in the
suburban Freihaus theatre. *The Magic Flute* is a
Singspiel and not an opera buffa or opera seria,
and was of course written in a language that the
ordinary people of Vienna could understand. It
was phenomenally popular, and even Mozart
was able to enjoy its success in the few weeks
that remained of his life after its première in
late September. In the first five weeks it was
shown no fewer than twenty-four times, and
Viennese publishers vied to engrave and print
the score. There were piano reductions and
transcriptions for string and wind ensembles,
and arrangements of music for dancing. Within
five years vocal scores had been published in Vienna, Berlin, Amsterdam, Bonn, Mannheim, Leipzig, Mainz and elsewhere. Variations on
popular numbers were later written by Beethoven, Spohr and other composers. There were sequels, including an unfinished version by Goethe,
and the opera itself established a permanent place in the Viennese
repertoire.

Yet *The Magic Flute* remains a paradoxical work. Commentators
have been baffled by the mixture of high symbolism and farce, and
Schikaneder's disjointed text has faced the severest criticisms. The apparent changes in the integrity and probity of the characters may appear
whimsical. The three ladies who save the young Prince Tamino from the
serpent at the beginning of Act I are servants of the presumably good
Queen of the Night who has lost her daughter Pamina to the evil tyrant
Sarastro. Yet it gradually emerges that Sarastro is the leader of a sect
devoted to truth, reason and wisdom. Instead of avenging the Queen,
Tamino ends up joining the quasi-masonic cult in the company of

Pamina, while the Queen and her followers are cast into everlasting night. The counterpoint to this elevated tale is provided by the earthy Papageno, who does not seek enlightenment but is only desirous of living peacefully in domestic bliss.

Schikaneder devised the text of *The Magic Flute* from a number of sources, including a set of fairy tales written by Wieland and an essay by the leading mason Ignaz von Born. He was not a dedicated mason like Mozart. Although he had joined the craft in the 1780s, he had been suspended for a period because of his disreputable behaviour and it is not known if he ever visited a lodge in Vienna. But Schikaneder was above all a man of the theatre, and deliberately devised a Singspiel that was not only topical in its presentation of Freemasonry, but included ample opportunities for spectacular effects.

The Freihaus ('Free House'), so called because it enjoyed tax privileges, was a large complex in the Wieden suburb, and was made up of several buildings surrounding six courtyards. It contained a chapel, dwellings for more than 500 people, shops and workshops of all kinds. The theatre was built in 1787, and was a simple rectangular structure with stalls and two galleries. Schikaneder came to manage the Freihaus theatre through a circuitous route. During the 1785–6 season, he had been part of the Burgtheater company but was too much of an independent spirit to remain in a subsidiary role. He separated from his wife

A watercolour of a stage setting for The Magic Flute *made by Johann Wolfgang von Goethe. Goethe was so enchanted by the opera that he planned a sequel which he sketched in 1794–5 but never completed.*

Eleonore and travelled via Salzburg (where he renewed acquaintance with Leopold Mozart) to his home town of Regensburg, and here he established a successful troupe for three years. Meanwhile, Eleonore went to live with another actor, Johann Friedel, who had leased the Freihaus Theater auf den Wieden. Friedel died in 1789, leaving her with the management. She in turn summoned Schikaneder back to Vienna, and he took over with great success. He staged German operas, comedies, tragedies, and spectacles, writing much of the material himself and assembling a talented company. Benedikt Schack and Franz Xaver Gerl, who played Tamino and Sarastro respectively, were both fine singers and popular composers in their own right. Constanze's sister Josepha was a leading soprano noted for her high range, and it was for her that Mozart wrote the Queen of the Night. Schikaneder himself was of course the first Papageno.

But whatever its virtues, this was not the Burgtheater company. The orchestration of *The Magic Flute* is therefore simplified compared with the da Ponte operas, and the woodwind are not required to show so much virtuosity. Mozart employed an extraordinary range of musical styles in *The Magic Flute*. The popular song style of Papageno's music exists alongside the fugues and chorales of the masonic scenes, the buffo ensembles, and the coloratura arias. This diversity has helped to ensure the continued attraction of the work [CD 3].

Mozart entered *The Magic Flute* into his catalogue in July 1791. The period during which it was composed was a stressful one, coinciding with the final stages of Constanze's pregnancy. In early June she was advised to go to Baden again, and she remained there for several weeks. The volume of letters from her husband attests to Mozart's loneliness and dependence on her. She first left for Baden on 4 June and Mozart visited her there on the 8th, but in the meantime he wrote her three letters. They are charmingly affectionate:

> Adieu – my love – my only one. Do catch them in the air – those $2999\frac{1}{2}$ little kisses from me which are flying about, waiting for someone to snap them up. Listen, I want to whisper something in your ear – and you in mine – and now we open and close our mouths – again – again and again – at last we say: 'It is all about plumpi-strumpi ...'

He did not like to sleep alone in their apartment, and since he had just dismissed their maid he went for a couple of nights to Leutgeb's house. After several days without her he became quite despondent:

> You cannot imagine how I have been aching for you all this long while. I can't describe what I have been feeling – a kind of emptiness, which hurts me dreadfully – a kind of longing, which is never satisfied, which never ceases, and which persists, nay rather increases daily. When I think how merry we were together at Baden – like children – and what sad, weary hours I am spending here! Even my work gives me no pleasure because I am accustomed to stop working now and then and exchange a few words with you.

Although her replies have not been preserved, she seems to have written to him with similar sentiments. Mozart visited Baden frequently, finding time in June to compose the exquisite miniature *Ave verum corpus* (K618) for his friend the local choirmaster [CD 3]. Constanze's pregnancy ended on 26 July with the birth of a son, Franz, only the second child to survive infancy. Back in Vienna, Mozart was getting up around five o'clock so as to start composing early in the day. The work strain was compounded in July when he was offered a new and pressing commission in the shape of his last Italian opera, *La clemenza di Tito*.

Tito: 'The music very bad so that almost all of us fell asleep'

La clemenza di Tito was commissioned by the Bohemian government to celebrate the coronation of Leopold in Prague as king of Bohemia. The contract between the Bohemians and the Italian impresario Guardasoni was drawn up in early July and makes for fascinating reading. The first clause stipulates that Guardasoni secure the services of an outstanding primo uomo and prima donna; this was the most important matter. Secondly, he undertook to have a new libretto prepared, or failing that to adapt the text of the play about the Roman Emperor Titus that had been written by the great Metastasio. It is only after these matters were detailed that Guardasoni was instructed to find a good composer to write the music. The composer is not named in the contract, and with good reason, since Guardasoni had not yet finalized arrangements. Mozart

A stage design by Giorgio Fuentes for the highly acclaimed production of La clemenza di Tito *that took place in Frankfurt in 1799.*

was not his first choice. Salieri was the first composer to be approached, but he was unable to take on the commission because of extra temporary responsibilities at the Italian opera. The agreement with Mozart cannot have been reached until the middle of July at the earliest, so there were just six weeks to write the opera and for the performers to rehearse and stage it.

La clemenza di Tito is a traditional opera seria, consisting predominantly of somewhat static arias and giving Mozart limited opportunities to exploit the dramatic ensemble writing he had developed over recent years. It is sometimes thought that he was reluctant to compose in a moribund genre, but this is probably not the case. First, he liked opera seria, remembering with affection the period he stayed in Munich for

Idomeneo in 1780. The only reason he had not composed a serious Italian opera over the past decade was that the Viennese court did not like them. Secondly, Emperor Leopold was a supporter of *seria*. In 1791 he instituted sweeping changes at the Burgtheater, dismissing da Ponte and arranging for singers specializing in serious opera to be brought from Italy. A success with *La clemenza di Tito* would therefore have been in the composer's interest.

Mozart had to work feverishly to prepare the opera in time for the coronation in early September. Fortunately, he knew the Guardasoni company pretty well. The part of Tito was to be taken by Antonio Baglioni, the Don Ottavio in the first performance of *Don Giovanni*, so his music could be prepared in advance. But the primo uomo in the role of Sesto was an unknown Italian, while Vitellia was sung by Maria Marchetti Fantozzi, a celebrated soprano but not one with whom Mozart was familiar. The time pressure was so great during composition that Mozart may have supervised his pupil Franz Süssmayr in the preparation of many of the recitatives.

Mozart and Constanze travelled in the company of Süssmayr to Prague in late August. The imperial party arrived soon after, and *Don Giovanni* was revived at the theatre on 2 December in the presence of the royal guests. The coronation ceremonies themselves began on Sunday 4 September, and it is probable that some of Mozart's Salzburg church music was performed during the service. *La clemenza di Tito* was presented to the imperial party and distinguished audience on 6 September. It was not well received, but given the rush of its preparation it would have been surprising if it had been a success. The problem was compounded by the fact that the court had an acknowledged aversion to Mozart's music. This was actually used as an argument in a later dispute over whether the impresario Guardasoni should be compensated for the poor box office receipts from the opera. Count Zinzendorf, that inveterate commentator on the musical scene, described the event as tedious. The Empress Maria Luisa wrote to her daughter on the next day: 'In the evening to the theatre, the gala opera was not much and the music very bad so that almost all of us fell asleep. The coronation went marvellously.'

La clemenza di Tito has been rescued from obscurity in the late twentieth century by imaginative producers and committed singers, and it is no longer seen as a museum piece. Its impact depends on the expectations of the audience or listener. Those who anticipate a lively ensemble work in the mould of the da Ponte operas will be disappointed. But in the context of the more sedate opera seria style, it is an outstanding work with individual beauties and a satisfying cumulative impact.

Success at last: 'What always gives me most pleasure is the *silent approval*'

Mozart and Constanze returned to Vienna in mid-September. There were still a few sections to be added to *The Magic Flute*, and the première took place on 30 September. Constanze was obliged to go to Baden again in October, leaving Mozart to enjoy the success of his opera. Although she was only away one week, Mozart's letters are full of news and delight at the reception of the opera:

> I have this moment returned from the opera, which was as full as ever. As usual the duet 'Mann und Weib' and Papageno's glockenspiel in Act I had to be repeated and also the trio of the boys in Act II. But what always gives me most pleasure is the *silent approval*! You can see how this opera is becoming more and more esteemed.

Mozart's letter dated 14 October is his last surviving one and gives a charming description of his activities, incidentally giving the lie to great antagonism between him and Salieri:

> Hofer drove out with me yesterday, Thursday the 13th, to see our Carl [Mozart's son, then at a boarding school near Vienna] ... At six o'clock I called in the carriage for Salieri and Madame Cavalieri – and drove them to my box ... You can hardly imagine how charming they were and how much they enjoyed not only my music, but the libretto and everything. They both said it was an *operone* worthy to be performed for the grandest festival and before the greatest monarch, and that they would often go to see it, as they have never seen a more beautiful or delightful show. Salieri listened and watched most attentively and from the overture to the last chorus there was not a single number that did not call forth from him a

bravo! or bello! It seemed as if they could not thank me enough for my kindness ... Carl was absolutely delighted at being taken to the opera. He is looking splendid.

Soon after the opening of *The Magic Flute*, Mozart had begun work on the Clarinet Concerto (K622) for his friend Anton Stadler. The melancholic atmosphere of this concerto seems appropriate for a work written two months before the composer's death, but really owes more to the timbre of the clarinet than to any premonitions of mortality. This piece, perhaps more than any other, demonstrates Mozart's mastery of the sound world of each instrument; as in his opera arias, the composer always matched his music to the medium. The concerto was completed in October, by which time he was almost certainly immersed in his most mysterious work.

The Requiem, debt and death

Mozart died on 5 December 1791. Three great puzzles hang over these last months of his life: how much of the Requiem he had composed, the significance of a large debt that was the subject of a court case in November, and the nature of his final illness.

The commission for the Requiem has given rise to more romantic embellishments than any other episode in Mozart's life. The work was commissioned anonymously, and according to Constanze, the composer became morbidly superstitious that he was writing this mass for the dead for himself. The truth did not actually emerge until the 1960s when a contemporary document was unearthed from the archives. This revealed that an aristocratic amateur musician, Count Walsegg, was accustomed to pay composers to write works for him anonymously. He recopied them, then had the music performed as if it were his own. His young wife had died early in 1791, and the count decided to obtain a Requiem from Mozart in her memory. It is probable that the composer received the commission in the summer through an intermediary who would not name the patron. However, composition was delayed by the preparation of the two operas over the summer, so it was only in the autumn that he could have devoted much time to it.

Section of the autograph manuscript of the Requiem, showing the beginning of the Lacrymosa (the last page in Mozart's hand).

The Requiem was unfinished when Mozart died, and there is some doubt as to how much of it he wrote or sketched himself. After his death, Constanze was anxious to present the complete work to the patron so that she could be paid. She first asked Joseph Eybler, a young musician for whom Mozart had some respect, to finish the piece. But when this arrangement fell through, she turned to the inferior Süssmayr. She probably gave Süssmayr her husband's sketches from which to work, but it remains uncertain how far he was following the dead composer's intentions. It is currently thought that the early sections are wholly by Mozart, but that the later parts of the Lacrymosa, together with the Sanctus, Osanna and Benedictus are mainly Süssmayr's creations.

While Mozart was at work on the Requiem, a decree was issued by the Austrian courts stating that he owed 1,435 gulden to Prince Carl Lichnowsky. Because he had not paid the debt, it was ordered that half his salary as Kammermusicus should be withheld. This information was unearthed from the archives only a few years ago, and is puzzling. Lichnowsky was the aristocrat with whom Mozart had shared his carriage on his north German tour of 1789, and has always been assumed to be a supporter of the composer. Mozart's financial position was almost certainly more stable in 1791 than it had been for some years. Moreover, there is no record of this debt or the charge on Mozart's salary in the extensive legal documents related to his estate. He died less than a month after the court order was issued, and it is unlikely he would have been able to pay off such a substantial debt within this period. Perhaps more will become known about the significance of this court order in future.

Mozart broke off from work on the Requiem in November to compose the short but rich masonic cantata 'Laut verkünde unsre Freude' (K623) for orchestra, two tenors and a bass. This was performed at the inauguration of the 'New-Crowned Hope' lodge on 17 November, an event that was so prestigious that tickets for public admission were printed. A few days later, he was struck by illness and took to his bed.

There are few definite facts about Mozart's terminal illness, since even the witnesses were rather inconsistent about the sequence of events. However, there was no lack of medical care, and several of Vienna's most distinguished physicians were consulted. He was in bed for some two weeks, and his body became swollen and tender. He remained lucid throughout, and seemed not to have had fatal premonitions, speaking confidently of future plans. His thoughts remained full of the composition of the Requiem until near the end. Benedikt Schack (the first Tamino) is said to have sung through sections at the composer's bedside on the day before he died, along with Franz Gerl and Franz Hofer. The Weber family rallied round, and Constanze's sister Sophie helped nurse the dying man. According to her recollections, as she entered the chamber on the day before he died:

> He called to me at once, 'Ah, dear Sophie, it is good of you to come. You must stay here tonight, you must see me die.' I tried to be strong and to

dissuade him, but he answered to all my attempts 'I have the taste of death on my tongue already', and 'Who will look after my dearest Constanze if you don't stay?' ... The last thing he did was to try and mouth the sound of the timpani in his Requiem.

Mozart died just before 1.0 a.m. on Monday 5 December, aged thirty-five. His death was said at the time to be due to inflammatory rheumatic fever, but later medical experts have suggested he suffered from kidney failure that may have arisen from one of his many earlier illnesses. Certainly there is no credible evidence for the fantastic theories concerning poisoning or overdose of mercury treatment. His death was tragic in being so unexpected, cutting him off at an age at which many composers have scarcely begun to write mature masterpieces, let alone enough to justify a place in the ranks of the greatest musicians the world has known.

Aftermath

Constanze was devastated by the premature death of her husband. Help came from the unexpected quarter of one of Mozart's most enduring patrons, Gottfried van Swieten. Van Swieten had troubles of his own, since he had been forced from his position as president of the Education Commission by the reactionary forces of Leopold's regime. Indeed, his dismissal was officially confirmed on the day of Mozart's death. Nevertheless, he took charge of arrangements, and the composer was buried two days later at St Marx's cemetery following a funeral service at St Stephen's Cathedral. The most modest standard form of burial was selected so as not to increase the expenses on the family. This involved being buried in a linen sack in a communal grave, the precise location of which is uncertain. Although the procedure sounds miserable, it was common at the time, since the ever rational Joseph II had objected to the needless expense of elaborate funerals, and had tried to impose the simplest possible practices. After the service, the hearse was not accompanied on the three-mile drive to the cemetery, but this was also conventional at the time.

Mozart's estate was in a bad way, but not as disastrous as might have been expected. The three largest debts were rather appropriately to a

*Portrait of Constanze Mozart
by Hans Hansen, dated 1802.*

tailor, an apothecary and a decorator. His belongings included an extensive wardrobe, the usual furnishings, a billiard table, a fortepiano, and a large number of books and scores. His own priceless manuscripts had no value at the time, so were not even mentioned in the legal depositions.

It is wrong to assume that he died alone and forgotten. Mozart's unexpected death was reported in a Viennese newspaper on 7 December and was soon known as far away as Frankfurt and Hamburg. A cantata in his honour was composed within a week, and a requiem mass was given by the opera company in Prague that is said to have attracted 4,000 mourners. It is possible that portions of his own unfinished Requiem were performed by Schikaneder's company at St Michael's Church in

Portrait of Mozart's two surviving children by Hans Hansen, 1798. Carl Thomas (right) was then about fourteen, while Franz Xaver (left) was seven years old.

Vienna within a few days of his death. The Freemasons published his last work (K623) for the benefit of his widow, and a 'Lodge of Sorrows' was held in his memory. The oration was published, and praised the composer's character as well as his talents:

> He was a diligent member of our Order: Brotherly love, a peaceful disposition, advocacy of a good cause, beneficence, a true, sincere sense of pleasure whenever he could help one of his Brethren with his talents: these were the chief characteristics of his nature ... He lacked only the riches which would have enabled him to make hundreds as happy as he would have wished.

The widow and her young family were supported in other ways as well. In February 1792, King Frederick William of Prussia bought a set of early manuscripts from Constanze for 3,600 gulden, a generous gesture far beyond their actual worth at the time. Van Swieten helped with the education of the children, and organized a benefit performance of the Requiem one year later. Constanze was granted a pension by the imperial household, even though Mozart's term of service had not yet made him eligible. A monument was built by a fellow mason in the spring of 1792, and the first lengthy biography (based extensively on Nannerl's recollections) was published in 1794. The myths surrounding his life and death soon began to circulate.

* * *

Constanze Mozart proved to be an astute business manager over the next decade, mounting benefit concerts, selling manuscripts for publication, and undertaking a successful tour in the company of Aloisia. She formed a liaison with a Danish diplomat Georg Nissen, whom she married in 1809. They lived in Copenhagen until 1820 when he retired and they moved to Salzburg. Nissen decided to write a biography of Mozart which was published in 1828, two years after his death. Constanze spent the rest of her life in Salzburg, an alert and well-bred lady, dying there in 1842.

Two of Mozart's children survived infancy. Carl Thomas was seven years old when his father died, and was educated in Prague before being apprenticed in Italy at the age of thirteen. He spent several years attempting a musical career, but eventually became a civil servant. He lived in Milan for most of his life, but attended the Salzburg centenary celebrations of the birth of his father in 1856, dying two years later. He never married and had no children. The younger son, Franz Xaver, was born in 1791 so never knew his father. He had more success as a musician than his brother, performing the C major Concerto (K467) at a concert when he was only fourteen, and receiving a testimonial from Salieri in 1807. He spent much of his life in Poland as a music teacher and tutor, where he was in love with a married countess. He toured as a concert pianist and composed modestly, dying unmarried in Carlsbad in 1844.

Maria Anna (Nannerl) had three children in St Gilgen, but moved back to Salzburg in 1801 after her husband died. Here she lived frugally as a piano teacher before becoming blind in 1825. She and Constanze never had a warm relationship even in retirement, and she died in 1829 aged seventy-eight.

Aloisia Lange had six children with Joseph Lange, but the couple separated in 1795. She continued to sing throughout Europe, appearing in Amsterdam in 1798 and Paris in 1801. She then lived for a number of years in Zürich before returning to Vienna where she endured increasing financial hardship. In 1831 she moved to Salzburg to join her sisters Constanze and Sophie, and died there in 1839.

Emanuel Schikaneder continued to run the Freihaus theatre until the turn of the century. He subsequently managed the nearby Theater an der Wien. His business affairs then took a downward turn and he became mentally unstable, dying in Vienna in 1812. Mozart's other great collaborator, Lorenzo da Ponte, moved to London soon after his dismissal from the Burgtheater. He became poet to the Italian opera at the King's Theatre, and also ran a bookshop and printers. He was made bankrupt in 1800, and a few years later emigrated to America where he opened a grocer's shop in New York. He ended his life as the respected Professor of Italian at Columbia College (later University) in New York.

Music Notes

Symphony no. 29 in A major (K201)

It may seem perverse to begin this selection of Mozart's music with a piece dating from as late as his eighteenth year, a time by which he had already composed more than a quarter of his entire output. Yet the symphonies of 1773 and 1774 appear to mark a rather particular landmark in maturity, and show a consistent inventiveness that has placed them in the higher ranks of his art.

What sets this symphony and its companions apart from earlier works? There are several features, including the thematic inventiveness, a mastery of style, and the beauty and grace of the orchestral colour.

Most of all, the symphony has a satisfying form into which all the elements seem to fit naturally, and in which the technique is so unobtrusive that an emotional balance is sustained without apparent effort.

The A major Symphony is scored for oboes, bassoons and strings, and has four movements. As in all the early symphonies, the woodwind play a very subordinate role and are chiefly used to reinforce the loud tutti sections. All the melodic material is given to the strings, and the interplay between first and second violins is very striking in this work, as is the imitation between upper and lower strings.

The opening Allegro moderato begins quietly with a simple but magical falling octave and quaver figure leading to a second octave drop and so on in sequence. As with so much of Mozart's music, the structure of the movement follows the broad outlines of sonata form. This involves an opening section in the tonic or home key, and a second contrasting melodic group in the dominant key (one fifth above the tonic), leading up to the mid-point. The first half of the movement is repeated. Then follows a more harmonically adventurous section (the development), which typically contains conflict or even dissonance, with bold modulations and rhythmic variation. The music goes through several changes of key before leading back to the recapitulation. The recapitulation returns to the main melodies of the movement, but this time in the home key throughout. The second part of the movement is also repeated in its entirety. The music ends with a vigorous closing section or coda, in which all the instruments join together loudly, with several passages in unison.

Next comes the contrasting slow movement marked Andante. The first violins, playing with mutes, present an elegant four-bar theme. This is taken up by the second violins, while the firsts add high musical arabesques that perfectly complement the melody. Themes follow one another in abundance in a way that seems almost profligate. Indeed, Mozart's fertility in using beautiful themes became a source of criticism. Years later, when the composer Carl Dittersdorf was discussing Mozart with Emperor Joseph II, he complained that Mozart used too many melodies, so that the ear was only just getting used to one when it was replaced by another. For many listeners, the themes seem to flow out of one another, and it is sometimes hard to say whether a melody is new or not. A great sense of stillness and calm pervades the music.

The third movement is a Minuet and Trio. The minuet here is a vigorous dance characterized by a strong dotted rhythm and angular theme, while the trio has a contrasting flowing melody. As is conventional, the minuet is repeated after the trio, though in a shorter form than on its first appearance.

The Allegro con spirito finale is an exhilarating movement in triple time, in a fully worked out sonata form with a rich development section. The main theme is a transformation of the opening melody of the first movement, and involves exuberant upward semiquaver flourishes. In the development, the main theme is put through numerous transformations of key, and there is some very striking imitation between the upper and lower voices. The movement ends with a coda in which the orchestra plays in unison, bringing the symphony to a boisterous conclusion.

When Mozart was living in Vienna nearly ten years later, he asked his father Leopold to send this symphony to him so that he could include it in his orchestral concerts. Its energy, style and inventiveness more than justify the composer's faith in his early work.

Piano Sonata in A minor (K310)

Solo piano music occupies an important place in Mozart's output. Eighteen sonatas survive, together with seventeen sets of variations and more than fifty other pieces. In addition, he wrote a further five duet sonatas for four hands, and one for two pianos. Most of these works were written for Mozart's own use in concerts, but they are not vacuous display pieces. Instead, they show on a small scale all the grace and originality of grander types of composition, and the technical difficulties are subtle and unobtrusive. Since so much of the solo piano music is superficially simple, it has been the staple fare of music teachers for decades. Unfortunately for the aspiring pianist, these works demonstrate above all others how playing the correct notes is only the starting point for performing Mozart adequately.

The earliest works would have been played on a harpsichord or clavichord, but in 1777 Mozart encountered the fortepianos made by Johann Stein in Augsburg. He was absolutely delighted with the expressive possibilities that resulted from the improvements made by Stein, and in later years these were his preferred instruments. He particularly liked the 'escapement' mechanism that returned the hammer to its starting point directly after impact, allowing the string to vibrate freely. The immediate responsiveness of the keyboard allowed cleaner articulation and a light touch. In comparison with the modern piano, the sound is brilliant and even, with particular clarity in the lower octaves.

Mozart wrote the A minor Sonata in Paris in the summer of 1778, when the impression made by Stein's instruments was still fresh. We do not know whether the sonata dates from before or after his mother's death in early July, but its turbulence certainly suggests a state of emotional turmoil. It is one of only two minor-key piano sonatas that he wrote, and is startling in its passion. Mozart was clearly influenced by the *Sturm und Drang* movement that was so prominent in the 1770s, and Joseph Haydn too wrote several minor-key works over this period.

The sonata is in three movements, with a slow movement sandwiched between two faster movements. The opening Allegro maestoso immediately establishes the emotionally charged atmosphere of the piece, with the inflected notes of the main theme being heard over repeated quaver chords. The second group in the dominant is based on a contrasting flowing semiquaver figure, and has a smoothness that exploited the technical developments of the fortepiano. In the development, there are jarring dissonances and extreme contrasts between loud and soft passages as the music moves through sequences based on the opening theme. In this performance by Daniel Barenboim, both halves of the movement are repeated as specified in Mozart's score.

The slow movement is marked Andante cantabile, and begins with an expressive theme that is put through a range of subtle inflections and decorations. But the anguished mood is seldom far away, and in the development the music broadens into fresh drama over a deep bass accompanying figure. The presto finale is shorter and less elaborate than the first two movements, but the restless momentum is maintained in the sinuous line and urgent rhythm. In the middle of the movement, the key turns from minor to major for an episode that resembles a rustic gavotte or musette, but the change is transient. The sonata ends uncompromisingly in the minor key, a compact masterpiece of uneasy expression.

Quintet in E flat major for Piano, Oboe, Clarinet, Horn and Bassoon (K452)

This quintet was completed on 30 March 1784, at the height of one of Mozart's busiest seasons. It was heard just two days later at an orchestral concert in the Burgtheater that the composer put on for his own benefit. The concert included a symphony, arias and improvisations, plus the Piano Concertos in B flat (K450) and D major (K451). The sheer physical energy required to play all these works during the same concert was immense, and Mozart's feat is all the more astounding when one realizes that he had appeared at least ten times over the previous two weeks.

It might seem surprising that he should include this chamber work in a grand orchestral concert. However, his programmes were typically very varied, and the Burgtheater was not so large that small forces would be swamped. In addition, this quintet had a special place in Mozart's affections. When he sent his report of the concert to his father Leopold, he singled out the quintet as having received the greatest applause: 'I myself consider it to be the best work I have ever composed. It is written for one oboe, one clarinet, one horn, one bassoon and the pianoforte. How I wish you could have heard it! And how beautifully it was performed!' It was played again two months later at a concert held at the family home of his piano pupil Barbara (Babette) Ployer. The opera composer Paisiello was present on this occasion, and became a rare Italian admirer of the young Mozart.

Mozart was right in his high opinion of the quintet, since it was probably a most difficult work to compose. This was possibly the first quintet for these forces ever written, so he did not have any models. The temptation must have been to compose a concertante piece, with the piano as soloist alternating with the wind ensemble. But although there are sections of this type, the overwhelming impression is of a subtle interplay between all five players. The piano has sections of virtuosic passage work, but never takes over the ensemble, and instead is woven tightly into the overall musical fabric. It is no wonder that the piece so impressed Beethoven that he wrote a quintet of his own (op. 16) for the same forces and in the same key.

The quintet is in three movements, the first of which is preceded by a slow introduction which lays out the grand design of the work. The piano and wind alternate declamatory phrases, and a descending motif is developed on each instrument. The wind instruments play as soloists while also joining in different combinations (clarinet and horn, oboe and clarinet, oboe and bassoon) that provide continuous changes in texture. The Allegro of the first movement begins with a theme presented by the piano and answered by the wind instruments. The movement is full of subtle rhythmic variations, and much of the challenging piano writing is subordinated to the other instruments.

The slow movement, marked Larghetto, begins with the oboe, horn and bassoon playing a calm melody that is completed by the full ensemble. Then the piano begins an arpeggio accompanying figure while each of the wind instruments plays thematic fragments that come together in an atmosphere of intense stillness. The piano in turn has a chance to soar over the gentle wind chords, and there is wonderful interplay between the instruments.

The finale is a rondo marked Allegretto, in which the thematic material is presented by the piano and wind in turn. Rhythmic vitality is supplied through an alteration between common time and triplet passages, and late in the movement there is an exquisitely mysterious section in which sustained wind chords are set against rapid triple-time configurations on the piano. Just before the last return of the rondo theme is a cadenza in which all the instruments participate. Unusually, this is fully scored rather than being an improvised cadenza, although it retains many of the characteristics of an improvisation.

Masonic Funeral Music (K477)

Mozart was initiated into the Order of Freemasons late in 1784, when he was at the height of his popular success. From that time onwards, he was a regular attender at lodge meetings in Vienna, and participated fully in the activities of the brotherhood. He frequently performed as a pianist at masonic events, and also composed a number of works specifically for the masons. Apart from this work, all the masonic music that we know of is vocal, and ranges from songs with piano accompaniment to large-scale cantatas for soloists, chorus and instruments.

The funeral music was composed for a 'Lodge of Sorrows', a special ceremony to commemorate two aristocratic masons who died within a day of one another in November 1785. The ceremony was not held at Mozart's own lodge, but at the larger lodge Zur Gekrönten Hoffnung ('Crowned Hope'). It was a grand occasion, and included an oration that was later published.

Mozart used this opportunity to create an intense and moving meditation on death. The piece is only sixty-nine bars long, but in an inspired performance such as the one given here by Neville Marriner and the Academy of St Martin-in-the-Fields, generates an extraordinary solemn religious atmosphere. The scoring of the piece is most unusual, with strings coupled with two oboes, one clarinet, three basset horns, a contrabassoon (or bass bassoon) and French horns. The basset horn is a close relative of the clarinet, but with a lower register and slightly more reedy tone. This combination produces a sombre wind sound that is unique in his works.

The music is continuous, but is nevertheless in three sections, appropriately so in view of the mystic significance of the number three in masonry. It begins in C minor with a series of slow wind chords. Then the strings enter with a mobile counterpoint, and this contrast between passionate strings and solemn wind chords is characteristic of the entire piece. In the middle section in E flat major, Mozart introduces the Gregorian chant for Passion week, the Lamentations of Jeremiah. This *cantus firmus* would have been recognizable to listeners of the period, and effectively integrates Catholic beliefs into the masonic ritual. The tranquil mood of the chant is soon disrupted by the return of the plaintive string phrases, and the material of the opening section is elaborated. The last chord of the work is C major, suggesting warmth and comfort after sorrow. In writing this funeral music, it is evident that Mozart did not perceive masonry to be opposed to the Catholic faith in which he was brought up. This small masterpiece transcends individual creeds to become a work of universal relevance to death and grieving.

Rondo in D major for Piano and Orchestra (K382)

When Mozart left the employment of the Salzburg court and settled in Vienna in 1781, he became known first and foremost as a keyboard virtuoso. He played in the *salons* of the nobility, but the real opportunity to enhance his reputation came with the Lent public concert season. The piano concerto was the obvious form to exploit in large-scale orchestral concerts. Mozart put on his first concert on 3 March 1782, probably at the Burgtheater. He was advised to include several numbers from his Munich opera *Idomeneo*, since it had not been heard in Vienna. There was space for only one concerto, and he decided to perform the D major Concerto (K175). This piece dated from as long ago as 1773, but it had proved popular over the intervening years. However, he decided to replace the finale with a new rondo composed specifically to please his Viennese audience. This was the Rondo with Variations (K382) that is included here. As well as being a delightful piece, it gives a good idea of the style that gained Mozart his immense popularity in the early 1780s.

The original finale of the concerto was in a rather severe contrapuntal style composed in a fully worked out sonata form. This new rondo is very different. It is a sparkling set of variations based on a simple symmetrical theme. The music is straightforward and immediately appealing, with few modulations or harmonic complexities. The interest of the piece derives from the way Mozart generated such a witty confection, full of charm and orchestral colour. The piano part is virtuosic, though not in an ostentatious fashion, and allowed the composer/performer to display a wide range of skills: rapid passage work in the left hand, highly ornamented slow music, and long trills in both hands. The variations are elegantly paced, with a minor-key variant full of pathos, and a later decorated slow section balancing the lively momentum of the overall Allegretto.

The movement was a great success. Mozart sent the manuscript to his father in late March 1782:

> I am sending you at the same time the last rondo which I composed for my Concerto in D major and which is making such a furore in Vienna. But I beg you to guard it like a *jewel* – and not to give it to a soul to play ... I composed it *specially* for myself – and no one else but my dear sister must play it.

Such was its popularity that Mozart retained the concerto in his repertoire for the 1783 season, even though he had written three new works (K413–15). On 11 March 1783, he played it at a concert put on by Aloisia Weber at the Burgtheater, explaining:

> The theatre was very full and I was received again by the Viennese public so cordially that I really ought to feel delighted. I had already left the platform, but the audience would not stop clapping and so I had to repeat the rondo; upon which there was a regular torrent of applause.

Ten days later, he performed it once again at his own Burgtheater concert in the presence of the emperor, the nobility and 'an exceptionally large concourse'. During Mozart's lifetime this was his most widely-known concerto. As we listen to the scintillating music of this rondo, it is easy to understand why.

Mass in C minor (K427)

Mozart wrote an immense amount of church music over his lifetime. This is scarcely surprising, since he was employed by the ecclesiastical court of Salzburg until he was twenty-five years old, and an important part of his job was to provide music for the cathedral. It was long assumed that he largely abandoned church music after his move to Vienna. However, papertyping and handwriting experts have recently redated to the 1780s several unfinished large-scale fragments of religious music once thought to be early work. This suggests that despite living in a secular culture in which elaborate church music was not encouraged, he retained his interest in this field during his maturity.

The Mass in C minor dates from his early years in Vienna, and was probably mostly written in 1782. It was linked with his marriage to Constanze Weber in the August of that year. In a letter to his father, Mozart described a heightened sense of piety around this time: 'Indeed for a considerable time before we were married we had always attended Mass and gone to confession and received Communion together; and I found that I never prayed so fervently or confessed and received Communion so devoutly as by her side ...' He took the unfinished Mass with him when they finally travelled to Salzburg in the summer of 1783. He continued to work on the piece, adding wind parts to the orchestra, and it received its first and only performance on 26 October. It was not sung at the cathedral, but in the church of the Benedictine Abbey of St Peter. One of the monks (and future abbot) was an old friend, the son of the Mozarts' landlord Lorenz Hagenauer. Only the Kyrie, Gloria, Sanctus and Benedictus were performed, and the Credo (with its glorious soprano solo 'Et incarnatus est') was probably never heard. It is not known exactly why Mozart failed to finish the work, but he may have finally realized that it was unsuitable for use in church services, owing to its ambitious scale and elaborate scope.

The C minor Mass is a 'cantata mass', with different sections of the Latin text set as separate movements (as in Bach's B minor Mass). During the year before it was composed, Mozart had begun to participate in Sunday morning concerts organized by Gottfried van Swieten, during which the 'ancient' music of J. S. Bach and Handel was played. This experience almost certainly kindled his interest in contrapuntal styles, a development that was probably encouraged by Constanze's fondness for fugues. The C minor Mass contains movements set in archaic styles that hark back to an earlier generation, notably the 'Qui tollis'. Yet it also includes forms that were very up to date, particularly the Italianate arias written for Constanze herself to sing as the soprano soloist.

It is not possible to include more than a portion of this grand work in our survey of Mozart's music. The extract presented here contains the first three movements of the work. The Mass begins with a solemn and mysterious Andante movement in C minor for the opening words 'Kyrie eleison' ('Lord, have mercy upon us'). The instrumentation is dark and elaborate, with oboe, horn, bassoon, trombone and timpani as well as strings. The Kyrie is punctuated by a central section in E flat major, in which the words 'Christe eleison' ('Christ, have mercy upon us') are sung by the soprano soloist. Here the texture is more delicate, and the soprano line is elaborated by large vocal leaps and rococo decoration. The choir then returns with the 'Kyrie eleison' material to complete the movement.

The Kyrie is followed by a Gloria that is divided into seven sections, of which only the first two are included here. First comes an allegro chorus that hymns the glory of God in a triumphant C major, complete with trumpets and timpani. The music softens for the words 'et in terra pax hominibus bonae voluntatis' ('and on earth peace to men of good will'), before bursting out again. The movement ends softly. Then follows the Laudamus te ('We praise thee'), an allegro for soprano. This is really an elaborate operatic aria in sonata form. The coloratura vocal line requires virtuoso singing, and has a wide range from very low to high notes. The music emphasizes the adoration of God with vigour and animation. Altogether, the C minor Mass is a wonderful work that repays complete performance.

Sinfonia concertante in E flat major for Violin, Viola and Orchestra (K364)

Mozart's five violin concertos date from his youth and years in Salzburg, and in some ways, this sinfonia concertante for violin and viola can be seen as crowning the series. It was written in the autumn of 1779, when Mozart was still assimilating the musical styles he had heard in Mannheim and Paris. Concertante-type compositions were a speciality of the Mannheim school of composers and were very popular in Paris. They were written in a *galant* style derived from the Baroque *concerto grosso*, with its alternation between the small group and full orchestra. The form was cultivated in Mannheim partly because of the presence in the orchestra of virtuosi on many instruments, and Mozart was clearly taken with the genre. He sketched out a sinfonia concertante for piano, violin and orchestra which was unfortunately never completed, and fragments also survive of a work for violin, viola, cello and orchestra that may have been intended as a companion to the present work. The Concerto for two Pianos (K365), written within a few months of K364, fits into this genre as well.

The work is scored for an orchestra of two oboes, two horns and strings. The richness of the sound is intensified by the introduction of two viola parts into the orchestra instead of one. During this period, the viola was a cinderella instrument, being typically ignored by composers. Standards of musicianship among viola players were often regarded as poor. But Mozart was particularly fond of the instrument, often preferring to play it instead of the violin in chamber ensembles. It is possible that he planned the viola solo part of the sinfonia concertante for himself, with the disreputable Salzburg Konzertmeister Antonio Brunetti as the violin soloist. The dark hues of the viola add a depth and plaintive quality to the piece.

The work is in E flat major and has three movements. The opening is marked Maestoso and is grand in design. The orchestral introduction (or ritornello) is elaborate, with the rich melodic material closing on an extended crescendo over a bass pedal note that was the hallmark of the Mannheim style. The first entry of the soloists, playing a long high E flat in octaves, is startling in its originality, since they gradually emerge from the sound mass rather than being announced with a flourish. The soloists sometimes play together, but often enter into a dialogue, answering one another as they develop the thematic material. In the development section, the soloists throw off rapid semiquaver phrases in a vigorous exchange. Towards the end of the movement, there is a double cadenza that was written out by the composer. It is a model of the improvisatory style, brilliant but with moments of pathos.

The slow movement marked Andante is in C minor. It has great spiritual intensity, with the soloists alternating and intertwining in a richly contrapuntal style. The exchanges between the soloists rise from gentle conversation to passionate eloquence, and both halves of the movement end in a beautifully simple but poignant coda. The sinfonia concertante closes with a lively Presto, shorter and less intense than its predecessors. It is in the form of a rondo, the main melodic material returning twice with intervening excursions. Mozart uses variations in rhythm, orchestral texture, and some thrilling writing for the soloists, to sustain the exhilarating tone to the end.

The Marriage of Figaro Act II Finale

The Marriage of Figaro is such a popular opera that it runs the risk of being taken for granted. In many ways, its composition is one of the most remarkable feats in the whole of music. It was written during the period of Mozart's greatest popularity, amid a string of orchestral and chamber masterpieces. However, he had not written a complete Italian comic opera since he was an adolescent. The demands of the genre were complex, and the composition of a handful of arias and scenes for interpolation in other musicians' work was slight preparation. Few composers managed successfully to bridge the gap between instrumental and operatic styles, and to write effective works in both fields. One might therefore have predicted that *Figaro*, as Mozart's first mature foray into opera buffa, would show signs of strain, and imperfections that would reflect his inexperience. Yet the fact is that Mozart solved the immense technical problems of the form straight away, and created a complex musical-dramatic structure that is unsurpassed in the operatic repertoire. He did not do this by copying the popular Italian composers of the time with their simple but appealing melodies and harmonies. Instead, he transferred his experience of the dramatic vitality of instrumental sonata forms on to the stage, so that the emotional tension of the action was embodied in the music. In addition, he exploited the abilities of wind instrument players to a greater extent than his contemporaries, so as to produce a much more vivid sound.

Of all the elements of an opera buffa, the hardest to pull off was the finale. The finale was an extended uninterrupted musical span in which there was typically a great deal of stage incident. The action of the Act II finale of *Figaro* is more complex than most, and Mozart embodied it in a large musical structure lasting more than twenty minutes. He divided the finale into eight interlocking sections, each one being individually characterized in terms of key, tempo and rhythm. Brisk episodes are punctuated by more sedate interludes, and the musical cohesion of this large span was strengthened by a logical sequence of keys, each of which has a clear relationship with its neighbours.

The Marriage of Figaro is set on the country estate of a Spanish aristocrat, Count Almaviva. The play on which the opera is based was the second in a series using the same characters. In the earlier *Barber of Seville*, Count Almaviva had successfully wooed Rosina with the assistance of the wily barber Figaro. Now several years have passed, and the Count is bored and has turned to philandering. Figaro is hoping to marry Susanna, the Countess Rosina's maid. However, the Count also has designs on Susanna and wishes to put off the wedding, so Figaro vows revenge. There are further complicating characters, including the ardent young page Cherubino, who has been dismissed from the castle and ordered to join the army, and the elderly governess Marcellina, who is in love with Figaro.

Act II is set in the Countess's chamber. Figaro has formulated a two-part plan to thwart the Count. First, he has sent the Count an anonymous letter asserting that the Countess will meet a lover that very evening. The Count is a quick-tempered and jealous man, and Figaro hopes that he will become so incensed as to forget about trying to delay the wedding. His second proposal is that Susanna will promise to meet the Count in the garden, but instead of going herself will disguise the page Cherubino to take her place. The Countess will surprise them, and the Count will be exposed.

In the numbers just before the finale, the Countess and Susanna have been enjoying dressing up Cherubino for his role when the Count comes upon them in a jealous fury. He has received the incriminating letter, so the presence of the half-clothed youth would be highly compromising. Cherubino is therefore hidden in the Countess's dressing-room. The Count is suspicious about the locked dressing-room, and his wife claims that her maid Susanna is in there. The Count takes the Countess off to fetch tools to open the dressing-room. While they are away, Susanna (who has overheard the fracas) quickly replaces Cherubino in the dressing-room, while the page jumps off the balcony into the garden below and races away.

In this extract from the classic recording conducted by Carlo Maria Giulini, the finale is preceded by a short recitative between the Count and Countess. On their return to the room, the frightened Countess (who is unaware of the substitution) admits to the Count that it is not Susanna in the dressing-room but Cherubino. The Count is furious, and begins the finale demanding that the rogue come out. The opening section is an allegro in E flat major. The peremptory commands of the Count, supported by *forte* wind chords, are answered by the pleading of the Countess. She gradually reveals that Cherubino is not fully dressed, and the Count's jealousy is fuelled still further. The music pauses unexpectedly, only to restart in the remote F minor as the Count disowns his wife ('Away from my sight, you faithless woman'). The home key returns with the Count's words 'mora, mora' ('He shall die'), sung against a rising and falling quaver figure from the clarinet and bassoon.

Their confrontation ends noisily. Then, as the door to the dressing-room opens and Susanna appears, a quiet falling phrase for the violins announces the Count and Countess's astonishment. The second section is in B flat major, and has a slow triple-time dance-like metre. Susanna's triumph over the jealous Count is sung over a delicate minuet. The Count cannot quite believe the deception, and goes into the cabinet to see if anyone else is there. At this, the finale moves into its third section and the tempo increases to allegro. There are busy quaver figures from the strings as Susanna explains the situation to the Countess. The Count begs forgiveness for his insulting behaviour ('perdono'), but the Countess refuses to listen to him. The women explain to the Count that he was being tested, and that Figaro wrote the anonymous letter. The Count continues to plead with his wife ('guardatemi'; 'look at me') and her resistance is at last overcome. All three singers join in a concerted section of reconciliation.

The mood alters abruptly with the entry of Figaro. There is a change from B flat major to the remote G major, and into a joyous loud triple-time rhythm as Figaro announces that everything is ready for the wedding. The musicians are warming up, and the crowds are gathering. But the Count puts a brake on the proceedings ('pian, piano, men fretta') because he wants to sort out the business of the letter. Figaro is put on the alert, and the Count realizes that he must play his cards carefully.

The music moves to C major for the next slow andante section. An elegant melody is played by the violins as the Count asks Figaro about the letter ('Conoscete, signor Figaro, questo foglio chi vergò?'; 'Do you know, master Figaro, who wrote this letter?'). Figaro flatly denies all knowledge ('nol conosco'), but is put into confusion by Susanna and the Countess, both of whom want him to admit that it was he. He continues his denials. He and Susanna renew their plea to be betrothed, and they are supported by the Countess in a magical passage sung over a sustained pedal note from the horns. The Count in turn pleads for Marcellina to enter to forestall Figaro's plans, and an impasse is reached. However, the mood is broken by the unexpected arrival of the angry half-drunk gardener Antonio. His entry is marked by a modulation to F major for the sixth section, a bustling allegro molto. Antonio is there to complain in a confused and inarticulate way about his flower-beds being ruined by a man jumping off the balcony. Figaro tries to laugh off the story as Antonio's drunken delusion. But when it is revealed that Antonio did not actually recognize the person, Figaro announces that it was he who jumped. Antonio mumbles that it looked more like Cherubino, but Figaro asserts that the page has ridden to Seville. 'I certainly didn't see a horse jumping down,' remarks Antonio, and the Count loses patience with him. Figaro embroiders his story by bringing in the idea that he hurt his foot when jumping. As he explains this, the music moves delightfully to a limping triple-time andante in B flat major.

All is not resolved, however, because Antonio now reveals a letter that was dropped by the fleeing figure. The Count seizes the document, and Figaro realizes he is in trouble. The gardener is dismissed and the Count confronts Figaro. The triple-time figure of Figaro's limp now takes a sinister turn. This interrogation section is a marvel of delicate interplay between the voices and tonal modulations in the orchestra. The Countess surreptitiously discovers that the paper is Cherubino's military commission, and passes the information by Susanna to Figaro. The Count then asks his servant why he has got it. Playing for time, Figaro sings 'Vi manca ... ' ('It lacked ... '), but cannot complete the sentence. The Countess realizes the commission ought to have the Almaviva seal, and when this information is passed to Figaro the music moves towards the dominant as Figaro triumphantly outwits his employer. The Count voices his frustration in a concerted passage while the others express their relief.

The mood shifts once more to a boisterous allegro for the last section. This is set in E flat major, the home key of the entire finale. Marcellina and her associates Basilio and Bartolo enter, demanding justice. She reveals that she has a contract in which Figaro promised to marry her if he defaulted on his debts. The pace moves up a notch to 'più allegro' as one block of triumphant voices (Marcellina, Basilio, the Count and Bartolo) take turns with the despondent trio of Susanna, the Countess and Figaro. The turmoil alternates with quieter moments in great variety, while never leaving the home key of E flat. The finale closes with a prestissimo in which Susanna, the Countess and Figaro sing a fast rising phrase in unison with the orchestra, cursing the devil for bringing Marcellina and her companions on the scene. General confusion reigns as the act comes to a tumultuous close.

Piano Concerto no. 23 in A major (K488)

Mozart's development of the piano concerto represents one of his most original contributions to music. His achievement was to fuse the concertante style of an earlier generation with symphonic musical thought based on the harmonic structures of sonata form. The result was a type of instrumental composition in which a whole range of dramatic emotions could be expressed within an ordered symmetrical framework.

The most fertile period of concerto writing was between 1784 and 1786, when he wrote twelve works that established the piano concerto as a major musical genre. These concertos share certain characteristics such as beauty of sound, inventiveness of melody and orchestration, and an encapsulation of diverse moods within a concentrated time span. Above all, they have a sense of harmony and 'rightness' that is characteristic of great art.

I have chosen the A major Concerto (K488) to illustrate the genre, since in many ways it is the quintessential concerto. It is a work that contains drama, humour, sadness and great warmth. It is the only concerto to have been scored for an orchestra that does not include oboes. The clarinet substitutes for the oboe, replacing a bright woodwind sound with mellow and darker hues. It is also unusual in having the first-movement cadenza written into the full score. Mozart's normal practice was to prepare cadenzas on separate sheets, presumably after completion of the rest of the movement. It is in Mozart's cadenzas that we probably come closest to hearing the improvisations for which he was famous. Contemporaries were astonished by the variety and inventiveness of his improvisations, but also by the way they fitted together so smoothly, and had such a neat and ordered structure. Rumours circulated in Vienna that they were not real improvisations but were worked out beforehand. On one occasion, scepticism was expressed by the organist and composer Albrechtsberger, so Mozart challenged him to present a theme. According to an observer:

> Mozart sat down and improvised on this theme for an hour in such a way as to excite general admiration and show by means of variations and fugues (in which he never departed from the theme) that he was master of every aspect of the musician's art. Albrechtsberger was so delighted that he was now fully convinced that Mozart had no need to prepare himself for an extemporized improvisation.

The concerto is dated 2 March 1786, so was presumably intended for the Lent concert season. Studies of the original manuscript have shown that the opening section of the first movement dates from at least eighteen months earlier, so it is probable that the work was sketched in 1784, and taken up again later. Interestingly, this first fragment included oboes in the orchestra, but they were replaced by the clarinets when the music was revived.

The concerto is in three movements. The opening Allegro begins quietly with the orchestral exposition of the main themes. When the piano enters, it does not simply reproduce the material of the opening, but enters into a full dialogue with the orchestra. The flute, clarinet and bassoon play important roles as soloists, and as a woodwind block set against the strings. The end of the exposition is exceptional in that it is interrupted by a new theme that is then elaborated in the development. The result is that the movement progresses seamlessly from one harmonic section to another with no clear junctions.

The slow movement is an Adagio in the unusual key of F sharp minor. It has been described as an outpouring of grief and despair, and is pervaded by an atmosphere of wistful melancholy. The apparently simple opening theme is played by the piano alone, and the orchestra replies with a poignant series of phrases taken up by the different instruments successively. There is an exquisite central section in which the flute and clarinet present a new theme accompanied by clarinet arpeggios in a deep register, before the return of the opening material in more decorated form.

The finale of this concerto is marked Allegro assai, and is one of the most delightful and colourful movements that Mozart ever wrote. It reminds us that the concerto was conceived around the time that Mozart was composing *The Marriage of Figaro*. The lively style, tunefulness and the interplay between the instruments bring the stage irresistibly to mind. Themes appear to flow naturally from one another in a consistently imaginative and diverting manner, rounding off the work in high spirits.

String Quintet in D major (K593)

Mozart's chamber music for strings covers an immense musical and emotional range, from the early divertimento-like quartets written in Italy to the profound mastery of the works dedicated to Haydn in 1785. As well as writing twenty-three quartets, he composed a marvellous Trio for Violin, Viola and Cello (K563), and six quintets in which a second viola is added to the conventional quartet.

The string chamber music is represented here by a late masterpiece, the Quintet in D major (K593). It was completed in December 1790, shortly after Mozart had returned from the coronation celebrations for Emperor Leopold II in Frankfurt. The piece may have been composed for Johann Tost, a former violinist of the Esterházy orchestra who had become a wealthy man of leisure. It was first played by an ensemble that included Joseph Haydn as well as Mozart, shortly before Haydn left on his first visit to England.

The quintet is written in the refined style that Mozart developed in his last years. The texture is more sparse and concise than in earlier works, with fewer themes and a greater use of contrapuntal and chromatic idioms. Over the years, the composer became increasingly concerned with the overall unity of his works, and with establishing harmonic, rhythmic or melodic links between movements. This is very striking in the D major Quintet, which inhabits a unique sound world, and while being written with Mozart's usual grace, appears almost experimental at times.

There are four movements, but the opening Allegro is preceded by a short larghetto introduction. The cello plays a series of spread chords that are answered by an ensemble of the other instruments in a brooding atmosphere of uneasy calm. The mood changes abruptly with the brisk Allegro which alternates delicate detached phrases with vigorous motifs, *sforzandos* and tutti chords. A unique feature of the movement is the reappearance of the introductory larghetto as a coda, enhancing the cohesion and unity of the overall musical argument.

The slow movement is marked Adagio rather than Mozart's usual Andante. The thematic material is new, yet related harmonically to that of the first movement, and the atmosphere is passionate and anguished. The cello plays an important role contrasting with the higher strings, but the first viola is also prominent in its interplay with the violin. The climax involves an exquisite hushed episode in which high decorative figures on the violins are played above sustained viola chords and *pizzicato* cello. At the close of the movement the music becomes more serene and tranquil. Then follows the Minuet and Trio, one of the most impressive ever written by Mozart. The theme is based on falling thirds, and there is a great deal of canonic exchange between the voices which gives a sense of irregularity to the rhythm. The contrasting trio involves an elegant dialogue between the two violins over pizzicato accompaniment.

The finale is an Allegro in triple time. The light, delicate and highly chromatic main theme was slightly altered by an early publisher, probably because it was thought to be too difficult. The original is reinstated in this recording. The movement includes elaborate passages of fugal writing and polyphony, with great rhythmic subtlety and a harmonic adventurousness that goes well beyond the normal bounds of a finale. The music races along without pausing for breath, rounding off a work that combines technical virtuosity with profound but uneasy emotion.

This thoughtful and exciting performance by Hausmusik is played on period instruments. The term refers not so much to the age of the instruments themselves, since string players have always coveted the products of early instrument makers. Rather it concerns the types of bows, strings and the performance style. The sound is smaller and less silky than with modern technique. The use of vibrato is limited, and the articulation of the notes is very clear with a definite attack. The timbre of the different instruments is distinct as opposed to the blended sound of the modern ensemble. Many listeners have come to favour this performance style over recent years, not only because it is closer to what Mozart would have heard, but also because it brings out new subtleties in the music.

The Magic Flute – Sequence from Act I

The music of *The Magic Flute* is so diverse that it is impossible to encapsulate within a brief extract. The opera was written for Schikaneder's suburban Freihaus theatre. The repertoire was catholic, with serious plays by Schiller and Goethe as well as comedies and spectacles devised by Schikaneder himself. However, the musical contributions were generally light operas in the vernacular, so Mozart was no doubt encouraged to compose simple melodious music that would appeal to the bourgeois audience. Mozart did adopt a popular style for many numbers, but also included solemn music for the quasi-masonic sections, together with bravura arias.

This sequence presented here has been selected to illustrate many of the moods and styles of the opera. Instead of picking out highlights, I have chosen a continuous section from the middle of Act I. It includes an aria along with ensembles, and introduces most of the main characters of the opera. The action that precedes this extract can be briefly summarized. The curtain opens on a rocky landscape into which Prince Tamino stumbles, pursued by a serpent. As he faints in terror, the Three Ladies (attendants on the Queen of the Night) emerge from a temple and kill the serpent. They admire the beauty of the youth, then go off to inform their Queen. The cheerful, feckless bird-catcher Papageno enters and sings a merry song about his life. Papageno tells Prince Tamino something of the mysterious country into which he has wandered, then takes credit for killing the serpent. The Three Ladies return, and punish Papageno for lying by putting a padlock on his mouth. They hand Tamino a portrait of the Queen's daughter Pamina, and he muses on her beauty in an elegant aria.

The Ladies return to inform him that Pamina has been captured by the demonic Sarastro, and that the Queen has chosen him as her rescuer. As Tamino prepares to set out on his adventure, the Queen of the Night herself appears. Our extract begins at this point, with an accompanied recitative for the Queen, followed by her aria 'Zum Leiden bin ich auserkoren'.

There is a clap of thunder as the Three Ladies announce the Queen's arrival ('Sie kommt!'; 'She comes!'). There is a ten-bar orchestral introduction, and in the original production this probably involved a spectacular parting of the mountains and the appearance of a splendid throne. The Queen flatters Tamino, claiming that he is the only one who can relieve a mother's sorrow. The aria itself is in B flat major and begins with a larghetto as the Queen recounts the abduction of her daughter. The pathos of the words is underlined by the sustained viola line when she describes Pamina's terror. The music is highly expressive of the Queen's distress; it is one of the paradoxes of this opera that despite our emotional engagement with the Queen's anguish at this point, she later emerges as an evil force. The aria now changes gear for an allegro moderato section in which the Queen exhorts Tamino to rescue Pamina, promising him her daughter in marriage. She elaborates on this theme in a spectacular coloratura section for which the role of the Queen of the Night is famous, before disappearing, leaving Tamino bemused.

The next number is a quintet for Tamino, Papageno and the Three Ladies, again in B flat major. It is a miniature drama in itself, accommodating a range of emotions from broad comedy to ethereal mystery within a concentrated span. It begins with Papageno humming a theme, since his mouth is padlocked. Tamino replies sympathetically, but is unable to help. As the music modulates to the dominant section in F major, the Three Ladies enter and release Papageno. He expresses his joy at being able to speak, and promises never to lie again. Then all five characters join in an ensemble for the aphorism 'Bekämen doch die Lügner alle ... ' ('If all liars could be restrained in this way, love and brotherhood would replace hatred, slander and black gall').

The music returns to B flat with a new theme as the first lady presents Tamino with the magic flute (Zauberflöte) to protect him on his quest. All the characters combine *sotto voce* to praise the wonderful flute. The music modulates to the minor as Papageno tries to take his leave ('Nun, ihr schönen Frauenzimmer ...'). He is called back by the Ladies, who tell him that the Queen has decreed he accompany Tamino. Papageno is terrified, convinced that the tiger-like Sarastro will flay him or roast him alive. The music modulates widely and becomes highly chromatic during this section as Papageno expresses his discomfiture. He is only mollified by the present of a chime of bells. The home key of B flat major returns as all five characters join in admiring the gifts ('Silberglöcken, Zauberflöten'), and wish each other farewell ('Lebet wohl auf Wiedersehn'). However, this is not the conclusion, since Tamino and Papageno remember that they do not know the way. The response is a magical andante in which the clarinets and bassoons play a simple but beautiful descending sequence. The Ladies describe the three wise young boys who will act as guides ('Drei Knaben, jung, schön, hold und weise'). This section hints at the masonic atmosphere that is later to enter the opera so forcefully, and acts as a quiet coda to a magnificent piece.

The scene shifts to an Egyptian-style room in Sarastro's palace. The confusion of good and evil continues, since it emerges that the bullying Monostatos is employed as Pamina's gaoler by the good Sarastro. Pamina has just tried to escape but has been recaptured, and the music of the ensuing trio reflects the turbulence of this moment. The key is G major, quite remote from the B flat of the quintet, and the tempo is a rapid allegro molto. Monostatos exults over the distressed Pamina, who begs him to kill her rather than prolong her torment. As she swoons, delicate steps in the orchestra announce Papageno's appearance. He spies the maiden, and with a new theme comes to her aid ('Schön Mädchen, jung und fein'). He and Monostatos come face to face with a cry of 'Hu!' It is difficult to know who is more surprised and terrified – the feathered bird-catcher or the Moor. Each believes the other is the devil and begs mercy before running away.

Papageno returns after his fright and in spoken dialogue tells Pamina that she is loved by the Prince who has come to rescue her. In the duet 'Bei Männern, welche Liebe fühlen', they sing of the power of love to comfort sadness and bring joy to life. Particular emphasis is placed on the words asserting that the love between man and woman raises them to divinity. Mozart felt deeply about this duet, and may have seen it as a credo for his marriage with Constanze. It is in two verses with a coda that elaborates on the words 'Mann und Weib, und Weib und Mann'. The orchestration is quiet and subdued, with clarinets and divided violas, and has an almost religious sonority. As well as being an affirmation of domestic love, the duet also demonstrates Pamina's strengths and straightforward truthfulness. She plays a role in the drama of far greater significance than might be expected in a piece inspired by Freemasonry. Masonic lore did not hold women in high esteem, and they were prohibited from all but the most superficial aspects of the craft in most parts of Europe. But in *The Magic Flute*, Pamina not only undergoes trials every bit as demanding as those set Tamino, she also leads him through the final test of water and fire. The emphasis on the feminine, and on the higher sanctity of marriage, was probably inspired by Mozart himself. His own diverse, often inconsistent, character and beliefs are perhaps more faithfully manifest in *The Magic Flute* than in any other opera.

Ave verum corpus (K618)

The final work of this selection of Mozart's compositions is a small masterpiece of choral music. The *Ave verum corpus* was written in the summer of 1791 for Mozart's friend Anton Stoll, who was a schoolteacher and the choirmaster at Baden. The composer and his wife were staying at the spa village in lodgings arranged by Stoll, and the piece was performed at the parish church on 23 June 1791.

The motet is scored for four-part choir, strings and organ, and is short and unpretentious. Within this compact form, Mozart exquisitely articulates the anguish and sorrow of Christ's crucifixion. The combination of beauty and simplicity reflects the artistry of a true master, and his awareness of the profound significance of music for human experience.

Further Reading

The liveliest and most touching account of Mozart's life and experiences is provided in his own letters and those of his family. The standard translation is *The Letters of Mozart and his Family* edited by Emily Anderson (third edition prepared by Stanley Sadie and Fiona Smart, Macmillan, 1988). More factual information is presented, albeit drily, in *Mozart: A Documentary Biography* by Otto Erich Deutsch (translated by Eric Blom, Peter Branscombe and Jeremy Noble, A & C Black, 1966). This is a compilation of all contemporary documents and references to the composer, and information discovered since its publication is detailed in *New Mozart Documents* by Cliff Eisen (Macmillan, 1991).

In my opinion, there is no really satisfactory full-length biography of Mozart in English. Alfred Einstein's *Mozart: His Character, His Work* (translated by Arthur Mendel and Nathan Broder, Cassell, 1946) is a classic from the first half of this century and has many insights, but shows signs of age both in its musical tastes and social attitudes. The most recent large biography is *Mozart: A Life* by Maynard Solomon (Hutchinson, 1995). This is an up-to-date and comprehensive account, but is imbued with hostility to Leopold Mozart and gives the music rather short shrift. Although it is not a biography, *The Mozart Compendium* edited by H. C. Robbins Landon (Thames and Hudson, 1990) is an excellent handbook of information about the composer's life, music, and the historical background. There are also valuable books about Mozart's maturity, in particular *Mozart in Vienna 1781–1791* by Volkmar Braunbehrens (translated by Timothy Bell, André Deutsch, 1990), and two books by H. C. Robbins Landon: *Mozart: The Golden Years* (Thames and Hudson, 1989) covering the period between 1781 and 1790, and *1791: Mozart's Last Year* (Thames and Hudson, 1988). A collection of distinguished essays on various aspects of Mozart's life and work has recently been published from the proceedings of a Royal Musical Association conference as *Wolfgang Amadè Mozart*, edited by Stanley Sadie (Oxford University Press, 1996).

Charles Rosen's *The Classical Style: Haydn, Mozart and Beethoven* (Faber, 1971) is a wonderful work of criticism and musical analysis, and is one of the best introductions to Mozart's musical style. The operas have been particularly well served in recent years. Daniel Heartz's *Mozart's Operas* (University of California Press, 1990) is a collection of essays on all the operas of Mozart's maturity. My own *The Mozart–Da Ponte Operas* (Oxford University Press, 1988) focuses on the cultural and musical background to *Le nozze di Figaro*, *Don Giovanni* and *Così fan tutte*. The Cambridge Opera Handbook series includes impressive studies of many of the operas, including *Don Giovanni* (1981) and *Idomeneo* (1993) by Julian Rushton, *Die Zauberflöte* (1991) by Peter Branscombe, *Die Entführung aus dem Serail* (1987) by Thomas Bauman, *Le nozze di Figaro* (1987) by Tim Carter, *La clemenza di Tito* (1991) by John A. Rice and *Così fan tutte* (1995) by Bruce Alan Brown. All can be recommended for readers interested in particular operas. A comprehensive account of Mozart's symphonies is provided in *Mozart's Symphonies: Context, Performance Practice, Reception* (Oxford University Press, 1989) by Neil Zaslaw. Otherwise, few other genres have attracted recent surveys, although there are many books and articles of more specialist interest. A very useful survey of Mozart's early works is provided in Daniel Heartz's *Haydn, Mozart and the Viennese School 1740–1780* (W. W. Norton, 1995).

Chronology

DATE	LIFE AND WORKS	MUSICAL CONTEXT	HISTORICAL BACKGROUND
1756	Birth of Wolfgang Amadeus Mozart at Salzburg, 27 January, second of two surviving children of Leopold and Maria Anna Mozart (baptised Joannes Chrysostomus Wolfgangus Theophilus, 28 January). Publication of Leopold Mozart's *Violinschule*.	Gluck 42; Haydn 24; Clementi 4.	Alliances of Austria with France, and Britain with Prussia. Seven Years' War begins.
1757		Death of Domenico Scarlatti (72).	Birth of William Blake.
1758/9		Haydn's first symphonies.	
1759		Death of Handel (74).	Voltaire: *Candide.* Birth of Schiller.
1760	Mozart learns to play some of the pieces in his sister Nannerl's music book.	Rameau's last *comédie ballet, Les Paladins.* Piccinni: *La buona figliuola* (Rome).	Accession of George III in England.
1761	First compositions written down by his father.	Haydn enters the service of the Esterházy family and moves to Eisenstadt.	Rousseau: *La Nouvelle Héloïse.*
1762	Visits to Munich and Vienna with his sister and father, where Mozart plays at fashionable occasions.	Gluck: *Orfeo ed Euridice* (Vienna). J. C. Bach moves to London.	Rousseau: *Du contrat social; Émile.* Ossian: *Fingal.* Accession of Catherine the Great of Russia.
1763	First visit to Paris with his sister and father. Plays at Versailles.		End of Seven Years' War.
1764	Leaves Paris for London. Plays at court of George III. First symphony composed.	Death of Rameau (81).	
1765	Leaves London for The Hague.		Joseph II becomes Holy Roman Emperor, and co-ruler with Maria Theresa of the Habsburg territories. Archduke Leopold becomes ruler of Tuscany.
1766	Visits Amsterdam and returns to Paris. Thence to Munich via Switzerland and back to Salzburg.	Haydn moves to Eszterháza.	Lessing: *Laokoon.*
1767	Second family visit to Vienna. Mozart and his sister severely ill with smallpox.	Gluck: *Alceste* (Vienna). Paisiello's first big success, *L'idolo cinese* (Naples).	Sterne completes *Tristram Shandy.*
1768	Composes *La finta semplice*, and *Bastien und Bastienne* which is performed in Vienna.		Captain Cook's voyages in the Pacific (to 1779).
1769	Family returns to Salzburg. Composes first mass (*Missa brevis*). Leaves for Italy with his father.		Birth of Napoleon Bonaparte. James Watt patents the steam engine.
1770	Visits Milan, Bologna, Florence and Rome, where he writes down the music of Allegri's *Miserere* from memory. Composes first string quartet. *Mitridate, rè di Ponto* performed in Milan with great success.	Birth of Beethoven in Bonn.	Marie Antoinette marries French Dauphin. Holbach: *Le Système de la Nature.* Goethe begins *Faust.* Birth of Hegel, Hölderlin, Wordsworth.

DATE	LIFE AND WORKS	MUSICAL CONTEXT	HISTORICAL BACKGROUND
1771	Visits Turin and Venice, then returns to Salzburg. Back in Milan for the performance of *Ascanio in Alba*.	Grétry: *Zémire et Azor* (Fontainebleau).	Birth of Walter Scott.
1772	Composes music for the enthronement of the new archbishop of Salzburg. Composes 6 symphonies, 3 divertimenti, 6 string quartets. Third visit to Milan for first performance of *Lucio Silla*.	Haydn: 'Farewell' Symphony; St Nicholas Mass; String Quartets op. 20.	First Partition of Poland.
1773	Returns to Salzburg. The Mozarts move house. Visits Vienna, but fails to get court appointment. Composes first piano concerto.		Pope Clement XIV dissolves Jesuit order. Boston Tea Party.
1774	Finishes 5 symphonies (begun in 1773), including K201; composes Bassoon Concerto, 2 masses, first string quintet. Leaves with his father for Munich.	Gluck: *Iphigénie en Aulide* (Paris). Haydn: Symphonies 54–7.	Death of Louis XV of France; accession of Louis XVI. Goethe: *Die Leiden des jungen Werthers*. Joseph II's *Allgemeine Schulordnung*: universal system of education to be created.
1775	*La finta giardiniera* performed in Munich. Returns to Salzburg. Four violin concertos composed, and *Il rè pastore*.		American War of Independence begins. Pugachev rebellion crushed in Russia. Beaumarchais: *Le Barbier de Séville*.
1776	*Serenata notturna*, 'Haffner' Serenade and 4 masses composed.		American Declaration of Independence. Vol. 1 of Gibbon's *The Decline and Fall of the Roman Empire*. Adam Smith: *The Wealth of Nations*. Sheridan: *The School for Scandal*.
1777	Piano Concerto in E♭ (K271) composed. Relations with the archbishop's court deteriorate. Mozart leaves with his mother for Paris, travelling via Munich, Augsburg and Mannheim.		
1777/9		Rivalry between Gluck and Piccinni in Paris.	
1778	In Mannheim falls in love with Aloisia Weber. Under pressure from his father in Salzburg continues journey to Paris, where the current preoccupation with Gluck and Piccinni militates against his success. 'Paris' Symphony performed. Death of his mother in Paris. Returns to Mannheim and Munich.	Cimarosa's first big success, *L'Italiana in Londra* (Rome).	War of the Bavarian Succession (to 1779). Death of Voltaire, Rousseau.
1779	Arrives back in Salzburg. Composes *Sinfonia concertante* for violin and viola, concerto for 2 pianos, the 'Coronation' Mass.	Gluck: *Iphigénie en Tauride* (Paris). After his last opera, *Echo et Narcisse*, Gluck leaves Paris for the last time and returns to Vienna.	
1780	Performance of incidental music for *Thamos, König in Ägypten*. Receives commission for *Idomeneo*. Travels to Munich to finish the composition.		Death of the Empress Maria Theresa.

DATE	LIFE AND WORKS	MUSICAL CONTEXT	HISTORICAL BACKGROUND
1781	Performance of *Idomeneo* in Munich. Summoned to Vienna by the archbishop. Resigns his post at the archbishop's court. Lodges with the Webers in Vienna and falls in love with Constanze. Composes 6 violin and piano sonatas. Begins work on *Die Entführung aus dem Serail*. Piano contest with Clementi. Meets Haydn.	Gluck's *Iphigénie en Tauride* performed in Vienna.	Austro–Russian alliance against Ottoman Empire. Joseph II introduces religious toleration and freedom of the press. Serfdom and guilds abolished. Kant: *The Critique of Pure Reason*. Schiller: *Die Räuber*. Death of Lessing.
1782	First concert in Vienna. *Entführung* performed by command of Joseph II. Marries Constanze Weber against his father's wishes. Composes 'Haffner' Symphony, first 3 mature piano concertos.	Death of J. C. Bach in London (47). Birth of Paganini. Haydn: *Orlando Paladino* (his most successful opera during his lifetime). Paisiello: *Il barbiere di Siviglia* (St Petersburg).	Pope Pius VI visits Vienna. Montgolfier's first hot-air balloon. Laclos: *Les liaisons dangereuses*.
1783	First son born, and dies after two months. Unfinished Mass in C minor performed. Visit to Salzburg to introduce Constanze to his father, and to Linz where he writes the 'Linz' Symphony (K425).	Haydn's last opera for Eszterháza, *Armida*. Piccinni: *Didon* (Paris). Beethoven's first publication (a set of variations for piano).	Peace of Versailles. British recognize American independence. Joseph II enforces German language in Bohemia.
1784	Meets Paisiello, plays at the Esterházy musical evenings with Haydn conducting. Second son, Carl Thomas, born. 6 piano concertos composed, also Quintet for Piano and Wind K452. Becomes a Freemason.	Paisiello: *Il rè Teodoro in Venezia* (Vienna). Grétry: *Richard Coeur-de-Lion* (Paris).	Beaumarchais: *Le Mariage de Figaro*. Herder: *Ideas towards the Philosophy of Mankind* (to 1791). Death of Diderot, Samuel Johnson.
1785	Plays quartets with Haydn, Dittersdorf and Vanhal. Publication of 6 string quartets dedicated to Haydn, who meets Mozart's father (on a visit to Vienna). Composes 3 more piano concertos, the G minor Piano Quartet, and begins work on *Le nozze di Figaro*.		
1786	Production of *Figaro* in Vienna. Third son born, and dies after one month. Composes a good deal of chamber music, 3 piano concertos (including K488), the 'Prague' Symphony.	Birth of Weber. Martín y Soler: *Una cosa rara* (Vienna).	Death of Frederick the Great of Prussia; accession of Frederick William II.
1787	Visits Prague, where an opera is commissioned. Back in Vienna composes *Don Giovanni*, produced in Prague on a second visit. Appointed chamber musician and court composer by Joseph II. Death of Leopold Mozart in Salzburg. First daughter born.	Death of Gluck (73). Beethoven visits Vienna and plays to Mozart. Gazzaniga: *Don Giovanni Tenorio* (Venice). Salieri: *Tarare* (Paris).	Schiller: *Don Carlos*.
1788	*Don Giovanni* performed in Vienna. Piano Concerto K537 and last 3 symphonies composed, also 3 piano trios and String Trio K563. Daughter dies.	Death of C. P. E. Bach (74).	Austria enters Russia's war with Turkey (to 1791). Birth of Byron.
1788/9		Haydn: Symphonies 90–92.	

DATE	LIFE AND WORKS	MUSICAL CONTEXT	HISTORICAL BACKGROUND
1789	Visits Dresden, Leipzig and Berlin, where he is presented to Frederick William II of Prussia to whom he later dedicates a string quartet. Constanze ill and goes to Baden. Clarinet Quintet composed, and *Così fan tutte* commissioned. Second daughter born and dies.	Paisiello: *Nina, ossia La pazza per amore* (Naples).	French Revolution. Storming of the Bastille. Proclamation of *liberté, égalité, fraternité*. Revolution in the Austrian Netherlands (suppressed 1790). Austrians take Belgrade and Bucharest. Washington first US president. Mutiny on HMS *Bounty*.
1790	Production of *Così fan tutte*. Stays in Baden with Constanze. Visits Frankfurt for the coronation of Leopold II. Visits Mainz, Mannheim and Munich, where he plays at a concert in honour of the king of Naples. Composes quartets and String Quintet K593.	Haydn gives up his post at Eszterháza and takes up permanent residence in Vienna. Salieri retires as director of the Court Opera.	Hungarian revolt. Death of Joseph II; accession of his brother, Leopold II.
1791	Composes last piano concerto, last string quintet, *Ave verum corpus*. Constanze in Baden again. Son, Franz Xaver Wolfgang, born. Composition of *Die Zauberflöte*, commission for the Requiem and for *La clemenza di Tito*. Goes to Prague for composition and production of *Clemenza*. Returns to Vienna, composes Clarinet Concerto and directs first performance of *Die Zauberflöte*. Health rapidly deteriorating, works feverishly on the Requiem which he leaves unfinished at his death on 5 December.	Birth of Meyerbeer. Haydn's first visit to London: Symphonies 95 and 96.	Proclamation of new constitution in France; Legislative Assembly. Boswell: *Life of Samuel Johnson*.
1792		Beethoven arrives in Vienna to study with Haydn. Cimarosa: *Il matrimonio segreto* (Vienna). Birth of Rossini.	Death of Emperor Leopold II. French declare war on Austria. France declared a republic. Thomas Paine: *The Rights of Man*. Birth of Shelley. Death of Joshua Reynolds.

Index

Page numbers in *italics* refer to illustrations

Acknowledgements

The Publishers gratefully acknowledge permission given by the following to reproduce illustrations and photographs: AKG London for viii & 3 & 26 (Kunsthistorisches Museum, Vienna), 6 & 7 & 65 & 81 & 165 & 166 (Internationale Stiftung Mozarteum, Salzburg), 9 (Museum Carolino Augusteum, Salzburg), 14 (Musée Condé, Chantilly), 17 (Musée du Louvre, Paris), 26 (Akademie der Bildenden Kunst, Vienna), 50 (Residenzmuseum, Munich), 75 & 107 (Historisches Museum der Stadt Wien/ (75) photo Erich Lessing), 83 (Hunterian Art Gallery, Glasgow), 110, 123, 127 (Villa Bertramka, Prague), 153 (Galerie Gilhofer, Vienna), 155 (Goethe-Nationalmuseum, Weimar), 158 (Institüt für Theater, Film und Fernsehwissenschaft der Universität, Cologne); Museum Carolino Augusteum, Salzburg (from the *Kuenburgischen Trachtenbuch*, Salzburg, c. 1785) 2, 3, 4; Historisches Museum Frankfurt am Main 13; Greater London Record Office Photograph Collection 21; Accademia filarmonica, Accademia Nazionale Virgiliana, Mantua 25; Civica Raccolta delle Stampe Achille Bertarelli, Castello Sforzesco, Milan (frontispiece from *La vera Guida per chi viaggi in Italia*, Rome, 1775) 27; Private collection 29; the Trustees of Dulwich Picture Gallery 30; Scottish National Portrait Gallery 33; SCALA (Museo Teatrale alla Scala, Milan) 35; Victoria Art Gallery, Bath and North East Somerset Council 37; © Internationale Stiftung Mozarteum, Salzburg 38, 48, 89, 96; British Library, London 40–41 (Maps K96.50), 77 & 103 & 124 (Maps 183.s.1), 90 (MS Zweig 69), 92 (MS add.37763, f.57); Fototeca dell' Instituto per le Lettere, il Teatro e il Melodramma, Fondazione Giorgio Cini, Venice 43; Stiftung St. Peter, Salzburg/photo Bibliothek St. Peter, Salzburg 45; Bayerische Verwaltung der Staatlichen Schlösser, Gärten und Seen, Munich (Residenz, Munich) 47; Reiss-Museum der Stadt Mannheim 52; Private collection 57; Deutsches Theatermuseum, Munich 68, 70, 72, 73; Bildarchiv der Österreichen Nationalbibliothek, Vienna 69, 102, 114, 116, 142, 146, 154, 162; Historisches Museum der Stadt Wien 71, 78, 87, 88, 94; Kunsthistorisches Museum, Vienna 76; Royal College of Music, London 105; Musikbibliothek, Leipziger Stadtische Bibliotheken, Stadt Leipzig 132; Mary Evans Picture Library 130; The Board of Trustees of The Victoria & Albert Museum, London 134; Graphische Sammlung Albertina, Vienna 148.

Quotations from Emily Anderson, ed., *The Letters of Mozart and his Family*, 1966, reprinted by permission of Macmillan Press Ltd; quotations from Otto Erich Deutsch, *Mozart: A Documentary Biography*, tr. Eric Blom, Peter Branscombe and Jeremy Noble, 1966, reprinted by permission of A&C Black (Publishers) Limited.

Map relief (p. 63): Mountain High Maps, ©1995 Digital Wisdom, Inc.